Open Source Software for Digital Forensics

Ewa Huebner · Stefano Zanero
Editors

Open Source Software for Digital Forensics

 Springer

Editors

Ewa Huebner
Computer Forensis
Consulting, Warrimoo
NSW
Australia
ehuebner@computerforensis.com

Stefano Zanero
Dipto. Elettronica e Informazione (DEI)
Politecnico di Milano
Milano
Italy
zanero@elet.polimi.it

ISBN 978-1-4899-8328-2   ISBN 978-1-4419-5803-7 (eBook)
DOI 10.1007/978-1-4419-5803-7
Springer New York Dordrecht Heidelberg London

Springer is part of Springer Science+Business Media (www.springer.com)

Preface

This book is a collection of revised and extended chapters based on papers presented at the Open Source Software for Computer and Network Forensics (OSSCoNF) workshop, held in Milan in September 2008 at the World Computing Congress, co-located with the 4th Open Source Software Conference, and some new work purposely commissioned for the book. It is aimed at scholars and free software authors, researchers, and digital forensics practitioners; it can serve both as a research archival resource, and an introductory text. To the best of our knowledge, it is the first research book totally oriented to the use of Free Libre Open Source Software (FLOSS) in digital forensics.

The purpose of the OSSCoNF workshop was twofold. First, we wished to determine the specific needs in computer and network forensics that are best addressed by the use and the creation of open source software. Secondly, we wished to give the authors a forum to present their tools and the research work that went into their design and development.

Similarly, this book consists of two parts, the first dealing with the motivations for using FLOSS in computer forensics today, and the second describing a number of tools (some that were presented at OSSCoNF), along with their evolution and some more extensive explanation of the details.

Part 1 consists of three chapters. In chapter 1 Zanero and Huebner discuss the importance of open source software in digital forensics with the focus on provably verifiable findings, and on easing reliance on expensive closed source software. Chapter 2 by Huebner, Bem and Cheung is dedicated to the application of the open source software tools in computer forensics education at tertiary level. The authors argue that open source tools are more suitable than commercial tools, as they provide the opportunity for students to gain in-depth understanding and appreciation of the computer forensic process. In chapter 3 Bem explores the potential role of virtual environments in the analysis phase of computer forensics investigations, and proposes a method which may lead to a gradual shift to open source software.

Part 2 is dedicated to novel FLOSS tools for computer and network forensics, presented in five chapters. In chapter 4, Vermaas, Simons and Meijer describe the Open Computer Forensics Architecture (OCFA), an automated system that dissects complex file types, extracts metadata from files and ultimately creates indexes on forensic images of seized computers. Chapter 5 by Giustini, Andreolini and

Colajanni presents CAINE (Computer Aided INvestigative Environment), a new GNU/Linux live distribution that contains a collection of tools wrapped up into a user friendly environment. In chapter 6, Gomez, Rojas and Mata describe VALI, a correlation model based on the concept of vector clocks to generate graphs showing the relationships between the reported events and possibly discovering unknown attack patterns. Chapter 7, by Cavalca and Goldoni, presents HIVE (Honeynet Infrastructure in Virtualized Environment), a novel highly scalable automated data collection and analysis architecture they designed. And finally, in chapter 7, Bassetti and Frati describe the Selective File Dumper, a Linux Bash script they developed to extract all the referenced, deleted and unallocated files and to perform a keyword search in a simple way.

   We trust that you will find this collection educational and informative, and that it may encourage the reader to explore the existing FLOSS tools in digital forensics and to inspire future authors to create new innovative FLOSS tools for the forensic investigations community.

Acknowledgments

This book would not be possible without the assistance we received from others. First our thanks go to Professor Ernesto Damiani, the editor of the series, who suggested that we submit the expanded OSSCoNF workshop collection for publication as a book. We would also like to thank the people who help us in the review of chapters and served as a reference for the publishers. Here is the list of their names in alphabetical order:

Evangelos Markatos, University of Crete, Greece
Mattia Monga, University of Milan – DICO, Italy
Marcus Rogers, Purdue University, US
Siraj Ahmed Shaikh, Cranfield University, UK
Iain Sutherland, University of Glamorgan
Magdalena Szeżyńska, Warsaw University of Technology, Poland
Doug Wampler, Bellarmine University, US
Alec Yasinsac, Florida State University, US

And last but not least we would like to thank the editorial staff of Springer Science, especially Jennifer Maurer and Susan Lagerstrom-Fife, for the patience and understanding they showed us.

                                                                        E. Huebner and S. Zanero

Contents

Part I
Importance of FLOSS in Computer Forensics

Chapter 1
The Case for Open Source Software in Digital Forensics

Stefano Zanero and Ewa Huebner

Abstract In this introductory chapter we discuss the importance of the use of open source software (OSS), and in particular of free software (FLOSS) in computer forensics investigations including the identification, capture, preservation and analysis of digital evidence; we also discuss the importance of OSS in computer forensics

1.1 Introduction

As the world witnesses what has been dubbed "the Information Age", the need to investigate digital crimes, or to retrieve digital evidence to investigate real world crimes, grows exponentially. More and more often, computer scientists and engineers are called upon as expert witnesses, testifying in courts of law and trying to help judges and juries make sense of data contained in laptops, PDAs, cellphones and other digital devices.

Correspondingly, "digital forensics" techniques have been developed, to allow the scientific investigation of events related to a digital object. Following Carrier's description, this process can be described as the formulation and testing of hypotheses about the state of digital data. This is done through the analysis of digital evidence, a process which must follow proper best practices.

As it is well known from literature, it is important in the process of a computer forensics investigation to use only software and hardware which has been properly and thoroughly validated for forensic use [3]. In this short contribution, we will show how open source software is inherently more suited to fit this requirement than proprietary, closed software, something which has already been debated in [1].

S. Zanero (✉)
Politecnico di Milano - Dip. Elettronica e Informazione, Via Ponzio, 34/5 I-20133, Milano – Italy
e-mail: zanero@elet.polimi.it

E. Huebner
Computer Forensis Consulting, 324 GWH, Warrimoo, NSW 2774, Australia
e-mail: ehuebner@computerforensis.com

E. Huebner and S. Zanero (eds.), *Open Source Software for Digital Forensics*,
DOI 10.1007/978-1-4419-5803-7_1, © Springer Science+Business Media, LLC 2010

The remainder of this document is structured as follows: in Section 2 we will define some key terms related to the open source software world. In Section 3 we will debate how open source software better fits the notions of scientific rigueur and validation required for forensic use. In Section 4 we conclude the chapter with the summary of the discussion.

1.2   Definitions

Throughout this book, we will refer to "open source" software defining it as any software which is distributed along with source code, or where any user can obtain the source code for no more than a reasonable reproduction cost. The obtained source code must be in the form in which a programmer would modify the program and must be complete and correctly build to the executable.

This is just a part of the original "open source definition" [7], still maintained by the OSI [10], which actually includes several other "rights" that a proper open source license should grant. This is in the line with what is advocated by the Free Software movement [9], and there are many merits to this broader definition, which is out of scope to fully review here. For the specific intent of this work, what we are mostly interested in is the freedom to access the unfettered, complete source code of a program or set of programs, in order to be able to study its inner workings.

However, it must be noted that several other freedoms commonly granted by Free, Libre Open Source Software (FLOSS) are relevant to its use in a forensic environment. In particular, the nondiscriminatory requirement, which asks Open Source licenses not to discriminate against any given person, group of persons, or specific target endeavor, is important, as it will be outlined in the following.

1.3   Making the Case for Open Source Software

What makes Open Source software a better fit for digital forensics? It can be traced back to the very definitions of the concept. "Digital Forensics", which can be broadly defined as "the set of techniques that allow the scientific investigation of events related to a digital object", have been formally defined by Carrier [2] as the process of formulation and testing of hypotheses about the state of digital data.

In the United States, the guidelines for reliability of the evidence are often referred back to a case in 1993, Daubert v. Merrell Dow Pharmaceuticals. As we have no legal training, we will not attempt to analyze such criteria and their specific impact in the legal field, but they are extremely sensible and they shine light on the requirements for forensic software, regardless of the specific criteria of a given state or jurisdiction. In the Daubert ruling, thoroughly discussed in [11], the U.S. Supreme Court suggested four criteria for determining whether science used in obtaining evidence was reliable and, therefore, admissible:

1. Is the evidence based on a testable theory or technique?
2. Has the theory or technique been peer reviewed?
3. In the case of a particular technique, does it have a known error rate and standards controlling its operation?
4. Is the underlying science generally accepted?

There is a tendency, generally speaking, in the public to assume that results of complex and obscure software artifacts are accurate. As observed in [12] this is particularly true for the tendency of courts to presume that forensic software yields accurate evidence reconstruction. However, engineers should know better: software and hardware have both systemic and random errors that must be appropriately illustrated to courts and lawyers, to ensure that trials and judgments are not biased by the "presumption of correctness".

If we analyze in a systematic way the testability (or better, according to Popper, the *falsifiability*[8]) and the calculation of potential error rates in any given software, we are confronted with two lines of thought. The use of open source software has been commonly recommended in the academic world [1, 5], since it makes every step of the reconstruction process verifiable, and makes it possible to determine the root causes of any error. On the other hand, vendors claim that proprietary software can also lead to verifiable results, provided that the manufacturer gives a thorough documentation and test cases demonstrating what their software does, and that the forensic community is made able to verify their claims. For this very reason, the NIST provides criteria for testing software and hardware for forensic use [3].

Both claims have their merits. However, we must note (following Dijkstra's famous quote) that while testing can only reveal the presence of errors, but not ensure correctness, source auditing can theoretically give a much more complete perception of the potential error rate. Also, calculation of error rates as discussed in [1] is actually much more feasible in the open source world.

It is also self-evident that, for the possibility of peer review of a tool, availability of source code and documentation is of the foremost importance. At a minimum, any software used in a forensic environment should be accompanied by specifications that document the procedures and the assumptions used in the algorithms, as well as details of their impact on the system, including the file systems. In most cases, in order to maintain the proprietary advantages on their know how, vendors will publish a bare minimum of the algorithms actually used to analyze the evidence, therefore precluding to the expert any knowledge of the assumptions taken and the potential errors associated. Open source tools, on the other hand, meet and surpass this requirement by disclosing all of their procedures through source code, thus allowing verification of the process.

Most vendors point out that the source code of their products is available, under appropriate NDAs and restrictive court orders, for review. While this is of course a good thing, the great advantage of having full access to the source code is that the experts can prepare ahead of time, and that the verification can follow an appropriate and scientific peer review path, with publication and disclosure of faults and defects, using the community effect that open source software generates.

As far as the acceptance of the technique in the community goes, both leading open source and proprietary software can cite great number of users, but this, as observed in [1] has little to do with an acceptance of the methodologies used. Once again however, open source leads on this criterion, because the possibility of open discussion and objection on fully published procedures gives at least the possibility to the community to object to specific procedures.

In conclusion, even if there are merits to the use of both types of software, it appears clear that Open Source has a large role to play in digital evidence analysis, a result which is also confirmed by a case study published in [6]. The latter work also outlines that the use of Open Source plays a prominent role in education of future forensic analysts, as it allows to understand in depth the techniques used for evidence reconstruction, something which is required for computer *scientists* as opposed to mere computer *users*.

A final aspect of the debate, which we didn't cover so far, is that commercial forensic software is often prohibitively expensive for small businesses and organisations, thus hampering their attempts to keep their computer systems safe and to recognize traces of illegitimate activities. Since all computer systems are connected in some way this has a globally negative impact on security and reliability of all of them. This negative effect can only be alleviated by widely accessible and robust forensic FLOSS software. Commercial software is also often prohibitively expensive, even under academic licensing, for colleges and universities.

Easing reliance on the expensive closed source software is of particular significance during the economic downturn of 2009 as shown in the March 2009 International Data Corporation (IDC) survey. IDC conducted one of the most comprehensive research projects [4] in the area of Linux adoption by large institutions (100 or more employees): they collected data from 330 organizations in different countries. It is reasonable to expect that with the growing adoption of Linux, the spread and the level of acceptance of the forensic FLOSS will also increase, further motivating the creators of FLOSS and encouraging more contributors to join their ranks.

1.4   Conclusions

In this chapter we discussed the advantages and benefits of the Open Source Software for digital forensics from the science point of view using the four criteria of the Daubert test, which besides being the guidelines for reliability of evidence in the United States, are also an extremely general and sensible criterion. We observed how open source software improves a correct evaluation of the results of forensic analysis, improving testability and avoiding an a priori "presumption of correctness". It also allows for a correct evaluation and peer review of the specific procedures applied to the evidence. Finally, Open Source software also improves teaching and research in academic institutions. All these merits are also further strengthened by the usual considerations on the possibility of lowering the costs and making software more accessible by the use of the FLOSS model.

In the remainder of this book, other authors will explore several different applications of open source software in forensic practice and teaching, and propose a number of projects that were nurtured and born in a free software environment, showing the vitality and viability of this philosophy in the field of computer forensics.

References

1. Carrier B (2002) Open source digital forensic tools: The legal argument. Technical report, @ stake Research Report
2. Carrier BD (2006) A hypothesis-based approach to digital forensic investigations. PhD thesis, Purdue University
3. Fisher GE, Computer forensics tools verification. Technical report, NIST. Available at http://www.itl.nist.gov/div897/docs/computer_forensics_tools_verification.html
4. Gillen A, Waldman B (2009) Linux adoption in a global recession. Tech. rep., Framingham, USA
5. Kenneally EE (2001) Gatekeeping out of the box: Open source software as a mechanism to assess reliability for digital evidence. Virginia Journal of Law and Technology 6(3), 13
6. Manson D, Carlin A, Ramos S, Gyger A, Kaufman M, Treichelt J (2007) Is the open way a better way? Digital forensics using open source tools. HICSS '07: Proceedings of the 40th Annual Hawaii International Conference on System Sciences, p. 266b. IEEE Computer Society, Washington, DC, USA . DOI http://dx.doi.org/10.1109/HICSS.2007.301
7. Perens B (1999) Open Sources: Voices from the Open Source Revolution, chapter: The open source definition. O'Reilly
8. Popper K (1963) Conjectures and Refutations. Routledge, London
9. Stallman R (2008) Why free software is better than open source. Available online at http://www.gnu.org/philosophy/free-software-for-freedom.html
10. The Open Source Initiative: The Open Source Definition. Available online at http://www.opensource.org/docs/definition.php
11. Tellus Institute (2003) The Project on Scientific Knowledge and Public Policy: Daubert: the most influential supreme court ruling you've never heard of. Technical report
12. Van Buskirk E, Liu V (2006) Digital Evidence: Challenging the Presumption of Reliability. Journal of Digital Forensic Practice 1(1), 19–26

Chapter 2
Computer Forensics Education – the Open Source Approach

Ewa Huebner, Derek Bem, and Hon Cheung

Abstract In this chapter we discuss the application of the open source software tools in computer forensics education at tertiary level. We argue that open source tools are more suitable than commercial tools, as they provide the opportunity for students to gain in-depth understanding and appreciation of the computer forensic process as opposed to familiarity with one software product, however complex and multi-functional. With the access to all source programs the students become more than just the consumers of the tools as future forensic investigators. They can also examine the code, understand the relationship between the binary images and relevant data structures, and in the process gain necessary background to become the future creators of new and improved forensic software tools. As a case study we present an advanced subject, Computer Forensics Workshop, which we designed for the Bachelor's degree in computer science at the University of Western Sydney. We based all laboratory work and the main take-home project in this subject on open source software tools. We found that without exception more than one suitable tool can be found to cover each topic in the curriculum adequately. We argue that this approach prepares students better for forensic field work, as they gain confidence to use a variety of tools, not just a single product they are familiar with.

2.1 Introduction

Software products have been used in university education ever since computer science and engineering entered the curriculum for undergraduate and postgraduate degrees. As the use of computer technology spread to all aspects of human activities,

E. Huebner (✉) and D. Bem
Computer Forensis Consulting, 324 GWH, Warrimoo, NSW 2774, Australia
e-mails: ehuebner@computerforensis.com; dbem@computerforensis.com

H. Cheung
University of Western Sydney, Locked Bag 1797, Penrith South DC NSW 1797, Australia
e-mail: h.cheung@uws.edu.au

E. Huebner and S. Zanero (eds.), *Open Source Software for Digital Forensics*,
DOI 10.1007/978-1-4419-5803-7_2, © Springer Science+Business Media, LLC 2010

various software packages also found application in teaching many unrelated disciplines. In the early days much of this software was created locally, mostly because of the non-standard hardware and operating systems available. Much has changed in this respect in the last 20-30 years as the hardware and operating systems market stabilised. For example in terms of operating systems, there is a virtual dual monopoly with the so called Wintel approach (Microsoft Windows running on Intel processor based computer) on one hand, and various distributions of Linux on the other. This duopoly is a good illustration of the dilemma faced by educators: should they use commercial or open source products, alone or in combination.

Academic communities always favoured free open source software. Cynically one might say that this is mostly because of perennial financial problems faced by most if not all universities. This is not entirely true as software manufacturers often offer heavily discounted or even free educational licences for their software to universities. This is not charity; students familiar with specific software products are likely to continue not only using them once they start their professional career, but also recommending them to others, increasing the market share for the producer. It is interesting to note that since 2006 Microsoft is offering the Windows Academic Program [10], which contains source programs for building the Windows kernel. This strategy has been obviously adopted to take advantage of this phenomenon.

It is our opinion that the preference for open source software in academia is based on the deeper desire for academic freedom and full control of the software tool afforded only by the open source philosophy. This attitude may have grown from early days when most of the software, including operating systems, had to be created in-house for the specific locally built hardware. With the growing complexity of software products it is no longer possible to maintain full local control over the software packages, and open source software offers the next best option with the possibility of local modifications, if necessary or desired. In comparison, a commercial product has to be used "as is" or not at all. There is of course the aspect of maintenance and continuity of the products, which is often seen as a drawback especially in the corporate world. This is much less of a problem in an academic environment, where people are much more prepared to assume a hands-on approach to software maintenance. The continuity is also not an issue, on the contrary academic programs are continually updated and new software tools are introduced routinely.

For students and academic teachers of computer science there is yet another incentive to use open source software. These students are future designers and implementers of software packages, and the ability to examine and manipulate the source of a substantial software package is an important part of their academic and professional development.

This aspect is even more pronounced for students of computer and network forensics. A professional forensic expert has to have complete confidence in the software used in obtaining evidence. This confidence may be based on peer acceptance of the product, whether open source or commercial. It is an important part of the university education for students to develop a questioning attitude and propensity for critical inquiry. Only open source tools allow the students to examine and analyse the actual code. This has several benefits:

1. gaining deeper understanding of the results obtained with the use of the tools,
2. extending the knowledge of the structure of the media and systems under analysis,
3. and, last but not least, a better appreciation of the construction of a complex software product.

We saw all these benefits realised in the delivery of the advanced third year subject, Computer Forensics Workshop, which we discuss later as a case study illustrating the application of open source computer and network forensics tools in tertiary education.

2.2 Computer Forensics Software Tools

The increased incidence of computer crime and the growing realisation of its potential impact on critical activities of the society created a need for dedicated computer and network forensics software tools. Commercial software companies and the open software community responded to this need with a number of software products which continue to develop providing new functionality and more sophisticated tools. There are now several dominant commercial players in this market, for example Guidance Software [6], AccessData [1], ProDiscover [14], X-Ways [24] and many others.

There are well established forensic software tools, both open source and commercial, for example:

- The classic Coroner's Toolkit (TCT) [29] – a selection of programs by Farmer and Venema dating back to 1999.
- The Sleuth Kit and Autopsy Browser [27] – an updated and enhanced contemporary version of TCT.
- Linux Security Live CD distributions – BackTrack [3] INSERT Rescue Security Toolkit [7], Helix [28], DEFT [5], etc.
- EnCase® Forensic Modules by Guidance Software [6].
- ProDiscover® Forensics by Technology Pathways [14] (Basic Edition is freeware).
- FTK™ (Forensic Toolkit) by AccessData [1].
- X-Ways Forensics by X-Ways Software Technology AG [24].
- Paraben Forensics by Paraben Corporation [12].
- NTI Computer Incident Response Suite by Armor Forensics [11].

A detailed survey of the market is beyond the scope of this paper. However it is worth noticing that this relatively new market is far from being uniform. Most commercial companies release a family of products with often overlapping functionality, and similar sounding names. A typical example is Paraben

Corporation who lists on their home Web page over thirty computer forensics related software packages [12]. This commercial policy creates a certain effect often not appreciated by the general user. To use a tool for specific tasks a computer forensics examiner needs to be trained in one of the commercial courses offered by a vendor who was selected by a company the examiner works for. After receiving vendor training in Paraben software a computer forensics examiner becomes familiar with specific Paraben terminology and their range of tools. Such a person is reluctant to change to another set of tools, as they became a "Paraben guru" within their organisation. This situation is very unfortunate and only serves the marketing purpose of one specific vendor. A company which invested in training their examiners in one specific computer forensics package typically has very little incentive to look at other tools.

This commercial approach contrasts sharply with what open source software can offer. Using any set of open source tools does not prevent an examiner looking at other tools – on the contrary, each new or modified tool can be easily integrated with the existing environment. This is of course impossible with closed source tools from different vendors. The open source environment encourages the examiner to better understand what a specific tool does, how it does it, and are there other tools possibly better suited to the task at hand.

While the open source environment has distinctive advantages, realistically one needs to appreciate that it would require a bold and unpopular decision within a computer forensics investigative organisation to change from Windows to Linux environment. In our recent work [26] we proposed an innovative approach where two parallel environments are used in a virtual machine configuration: the host (or the main environment) is Linux, and a Windows system is installed as a virtual guest. In such an environment an acquired disk image which needs to be analysed is mounted on the host Linux, and can be accessed at the same time from two environments: Linux and Windows.

A unique advantage of such a setup is creating a mechanism for natural migration between Windows environment and tools to Linux platform without "burning bridges": every investigator working in the Linux host environment with Windows running as a guest would still have full access to the familiar Windows tools. Moreover the investigator is not forced to use any environment in preference to another. It is natural that an investigator working in a parallel Windows/Linux environment would start trying Linux tools, and benefit from the new and powerful utilities as well as techniques not available under Windows.

2.3   Case Study

To demonstrate the application of open source computer forensics software in tertiary education we will discuss the computer forensics specialisation for the Bachelor of Computer Science degree at the University of Western Sydney [18] which was designed in 2005, first offered in 2006, and delivered annually. Our motivation for introducing it was twofold. Firstly we could see the rapidly increasing demand for computer forensics professionals, and secondly we wanted to reignite the interest of prospective students in computer science as it was in noticeable decline across the world after the Y2K bug and the dot-com crash.

We previously had a solid program in computer science with a specialisation in systems programming, so the groundwork on which to build a computer forensics stream was already there. Topics like operating systems internals, file systems, computer organisation, data representation, information security, computer networks and the operation of a computer system were adequately covered in existing subjects. For the computer forensics specialisation we introduced a new subject, Computer Forensics Workshop, which was designed from scratch to serve as a capstone for the stream.

To ensure that students obtained the maximum benefit from attending the workshop, we set prerequisite subjects, namely Operating Systems, Systems Administration Programming and Network Security. To obtain the specialization in computer forensics students also have to complete the following subjects: Computer Networks and Internets, Computer Security, Information Security, and a specialised subject dealing with law of evidence, delivered by the School of Law. This complements a generic computer science program, which covers all core topics recommended by the ACM/IEEE-CS Computer Science Curricula [2].

2.3.1   *Computer Forensics Workshop - Content and Outcomes*

Computer Forensics Workshop [19] is the capstone subject in the stream. It is delivered as a combination of weekly lectures and laboratory sessions. The hands-on component is obviously very important in a workshop based subject, so the laboratory sessions last for 4 hours, twice the time compared with other subjects. The assessment is mostly based on laboratory reports, which students complete in their own time. The reports are intended to reinforce the need for meticulous documentation of all investigative activities performed in the laboratory session. There is also an assignment, completed outside scheduled hours. Because of the practical nature of the material covered, we decided that a final written exam would not be a suitable assessment tool.

Unlike other fields in computer science, no guidelines or recommendations exist for computer forensics curricula, so we had to rely mostly on our own research and professional experience in the related fields. The same process was followed by other universities introducing computer forensics into their curricula at the time [30, 32, 35]. The characteristic feature of our approach was to focus on first principles instead of relying on specific forensic software tools. This was our motivation for adopting an open source software approach with the variety of forensic tools available, from suites of programs to single independent utilities.

The first topic we covered was media preparation and copying techniques, so that students understand the issues involved in the preparation of forensically clean storage media to accept image copies of suspect media as well as performing an image copy from multiple storage media types without altering the source media.

This topic allows for the application of manual techniques using the disk imaging dd utility [16] and industry forensic software suites.

The next topic was file system structures and file type identification techniques, analysis of time stamps as well as searching for and identifying hidden data. We chose to cover in detail the prevailing file system formats in Windows and Unix derivative systems, namely FAT, VFAT, NTFS, Ext2 and Ext3. Analysis of file systems is the mainstay of computer forensics, and we decided to expose students to all possible techniques, from direct examination of binary data to sophisticated software suites.

As a prerequisite to the Computer Forensics Workshop students complete three security related subjects: Computer Security, Information Security and Network Security. These subjects cover security issues exhaustively, so there was no need for a substantial security component. It was still important to impress on students the consequences of applying computer security measures, including cryptography and steganography, in a forensic setting. Again we attempted to expose students to a whole range of tools and techniques, and we were able to use many open source software tools for hiding and encrypting data, as well as analysis of such data.

We also introduced new computer forensics techniques like live system investigations and memory forensics. The former was also used to demonstrate how much information can be gained from the system without privileged access, and the latter to show that clear text including passwords can be extracted from a memory image. Naturally there are many tools for Unix derivative systems, including native system tools which are open source. There are free forensic tools for Windows [9], which are not open source.

Another important topic which has to be included in the curriculum is network forensics. This included, but was not limited to, analysis and reconstruction of network activity and web browsing, as well as extraction and reconstruction of emails. Again many open source software tools exist to support forensic investigation of networks, and we allowed students to select the tools themselves. We did it to encourage students to try new unfamiliar tools and to gain skills comparing various tools

The final topic was how to prepare a system and network to best support subsequent intrusion and activity detection. We wanted to make sure that students realise the importance of a forensic plan for any computer installation, and are able to formulate such a plan in various environments. This is different from securing and protecting the system, and deals with processes and procedures necessary for adequate incident response management.

2.3.2 Workshop Requirements

There are some technical issues in an educational environment which need to be resolved to provide a suitable laboratory environment for computer and networks forensics, as reported in [30]. Firstly, some of the investigative procedures require fully privileged access to the computer system. The best solution is to build a stand-alone dedicated laboratory with limited controlled access to the network to create a safe 'sandbox' environment. This was not generally possible in our case, as all laboratory rooms serve many different purposes, and it would not be economically viable to limit the usage to one subject only. One exception was the network forensics, as we had access to a properly equipped and isolated laboratory dedicated to teaching networks.

We solved this problem by using Helix, an open source customised distribution of the Knoppix Live Linux CD [28], which boots from a CD ROM and uses memory-mapped disks. The content of the local hard disk is never changed, and it is easy to restore the normal environment for the next class by rebooting all systems. We also designed the laboratory work in such a way that in most cases privileged access to the system was not required.

There are also various freeware products, for example Sleuthkit and Autopsy [27], which are packaged in the Helix distribution. To enable students to use the laboratories after hours we also installed Sleuthkit and Autopsy on the local distribution of Linux, provided in all laboratory computers by default, giving students access to Sleuthkit commands. Students were also provided with relevant URLs to be able to download the products and install them on their home computers.

2.3.3   Laboratory Structure

The laboratory experience plays a central role in a workshop style subject. Students have to be able to test the knowledge they gained by performing practical tasks, which in a professional setting would be part of a computer forensics investigation. Our notes below reflect the content of Computer Forensics Workshop during previous years, as well as changes and modifications which we are including in the latest 2008 delivery.

In the course of a 13-week semester we provide ten laboratory sessions, each preceded by the relevant lecture presenting the theoretical background and providing students with sufficient knowledge to be able to handle the laboratory tasks. In addition the assignments bring together knowledge acquired in individual modules, and help the students to coalesce the experiences in the laboratory sessions into one coherent whole. The following laboratory sessions are scheduled:

1. FAT file system investigation,
2. EXTn file system investigation,
3. Media preparation and imaging,
4. NTFS file system investigation,
5. Network forensics (3 modules),
6. Applied cryptography (2 modules),
7. Live systems investigation.

2.3.3.1   FAT File System Investigation

For this laboratory session we decided to give students an opportunity to examine the image at the binary level using a hex editor. To make the task less onerous we selected the simplest of FAT systems, FAT12. Students were given an image of a floppy diskette, and asked a number of questions regarding the structure of the volume represented by this image, including the creation of the human-readable representation of the FAT table. The answers were to be based strictly on a HEX/ASCII view of the image. The additional difficulty in interpretation of the binary data was the little-endian representation and the necessity to split some bytes into 4-bit nibbles for FAT12 structures. The students of computer science dealt with this task easily, but some of the externals needed time to recall the skills they haven't used for a while.

The product we chose was a well known hex editor - Tiny Hexer, a free tool provided by Markus Stephany from Germany. Unfortunately this tool is not developed any more and not available for download, however we have Markus' permission to use the last available version which is very stable and perfect for our purpose. In addition to viewing HEX representation, this tool comes with a number of macros, which help interpret the image assuming a number of file systems. Students could use the FAT12 macro to confirm their own findings. In the future we would look at other similar hex tools which could replace Tiny Hexer.

2.3.3.2 Ext File System Investigation

For the laboratory exercises we selected the simplest of the Ext file systems, i.e. Ext2. We based the student tasks on the excellent guide provided by Barry Grundy [31]. The guide provides a series of exercises based on a disk image with a number of partitions, including an Ext2 partition. There is also a log file provided, which contains output of various commands used while data was collected from the original disk. After determining the disk structure, students carve the image into separate partitions, and proceed to examine the Ext2 partition with a number of Sleuthkit tools, for example ffstat, fls and icat. Some native Linux commands are also used to examine tar archives and determine the types of files found in the image. As an extension of these activities, students repeat the investigation outside the scheduled lab using Autopsy.

2.3.3.3 NTFS File System Investigation

Again we based the student tasks on the same excellent guide provided by Barry Grundy [31], and we used the Linux environment exclusively to analyse the NTFS image. This session was the most difficult of the three dedicated to file systems, because NTFS is not only the most complex of the systems included, but the full NTFS documentation is not in public domain. It is thanks to organisations like the Linux NTFS Project [11] that more is known about the NTFS structure, and most of the features are documented [34] based on reverse-engineering. The analysis of the NTFS image is conducted using Sleuthkit commands. Students derive a double benefit from this session. Not only they gain appreciation of the NTFS file system, but also they see that it can be fully investigated using FLOSS tools.

2.3.3.4   Media Preparation and Imaging

The students were asked to acquire a disk image using two different approaches and different environments. The first exercise used the AIR (Automated Image and Restore) tool from the Helix live Linux CD. In the second exercise the workstation was booted to Windows environment and students used the "Capture & Add Image" option from ProDiscover Basic software package. The next more advanced exercise asked students to carve certain areas of data using ProDiscover Basic. In the Ext laboratory students performed data carving using a different image and the Sleuthkit open source tool kit. In this set of exercises the students saw that they can use close source or open source tools which are functionally equivalent.

2.3.3.5   Network Forensics Modules

In previous deliveries we were using a mixture of Ethernet connected machines separated from the university network by a Linux based router. The computers in the lab were organised into groups. All computers in a group were connected to a hub. The use of a hub enabled network traffic amongst the computers in a group to be captured. All the hubs were connected to the router via a switch. There were three laboratory sessions related to the three network forensics modules, respectively network activity reconstruction, web browsing activity reconstruction and email extraction and reconstruction

Network Activity Reconstruction

The lab tasks in this session required the students to create various types of network traffic on the lab's network. They included some network protocols, simple text files, document files, and image files. Students were asked to capture the network traffic and to perform initial reconstruction of the captured information to its original application format. An open source network monitoring tool, i.e. Wireshark [23], was used. Wireshark is an excellent tool in collecting data from a network and it has some facilities to help in reconstructing application data. For reconstruction of more complex captured data, a substantial amount of manual intervention may be required.

Web Browsing Activity Reconstruction

This session was on reconstructing web browsing activities from cached files in a user's computer, especially from cached files created by a web browser. Students were asked to create data to be collected and reconstructed, by performing a number of different browsing activities using the Internet Explorer web browser. The activities included browsing and searching, Internet shopping, downloading, and other popular Web browsing activities. Students were asked to select two of the browsing activities to perform initial reconstructions, by using an open source or freeware tool. No particular tool was specified, and students chose and downloaded the tool of their preference. Two of tools mostly chosen by students were open source Pasco [13] and freeware Web Historian [21]. In addition, students were asked to reconstruct some of the Web browsing activities manually, without the help of a tool, so that they could appreciate the differences between the two approaches and could improve their understanding of the inner working of the tool.

Email Extraction and Reconstruction

This session consisted of two major tasks on extracting and reconstructing emails from email storage files, and capturing and reconstructing email network traffic. The email storage files used in this task were the Outlook Express DBX files. Students were asked to extract several emails from the files, using a hex editor and guided by some knowledge of the structures of the files. The DBX files were intentionally damaged so that they could not be opened by the original application. The second major task was to capture network traffic containing a user's Web based emails and to reconstruct the emails from the captured traffic. Similar to Network Activity Reconstructions, the open source tool Wireshark was used to capture the network traffic and to help in reconstructing the captured web based emails. Different Web based email software products have different ways in composing and sending the emails. Reconstructing the captured emails involved a substantial amount of manual manipulations and knowledge of the underlining interactions between the web browser and the remote email server.

The current lab arrangement is adequate in providing students with knowledge in network forensics mostly on a local area network environment. One of the shortcomings in only using physical machines is that it is difficult to expand the coverage to an internetworking environment. Thus we intend to shift to workstations running virtualisation. Initially, a more mature commercial visualisation software, VMware [20], will be used. An open source visualisation tool such as Xen [25] may also be considered in the future. This arrangement should allow for setting up a larger scale and more flexible virtual network system within the lab without the need to physically expanding to the real university maintained network. It is possible in such an environment to simulate a wide variety of network scenarios. The only trade off is that relatively powerful workstations and servers are required to support such an environment.

2.3.3.6 Applied Cryptography Modules

The example encryption system used in this session was the Microsoft Encrypted File System (EFS) bundled with the NTFS file system. The students follow the methodology of extracting EFS decrypted files from a live system presented in [33]. The method of extraction is built around a free software utility, Robocopy [8] which does not modify any metadata of the file system during extraction. To confirm that this approach is forensically sound, students have to obtain a hash value for the captured data calculated before and after the extraction. This is the first time students are introduced to the concept of live system investigation, and they learn to appreciate that it is indispensable in obtaining complete information about the system being examined.

We are also currently preparing a series of exercises based on TrueCrypt [17], the open source disk encryption software for Windows Vista/XP, Mac OS X, and Linux. TrueCrypt is a very powerful tool which allows the creation of a virtual encrypted disk within a file, which in turn is mounted as a real disk. Another option which it offers is the encryption of the entire partition or storage device. TrueCrypt is particularly interesting from the computer forensics point of view as the TrueCrypt volume cannot be identified as hiding information because the data is very well randomised. We intend to make students aware that various commercial encryption breaking tools fail to recognise the TrueCrypt volumes as carrying encrypted data. What's more even if there is an attempt to decrypt the data, it is not possible to guess the key within a realistic time frame. In a practical exercise one group of students selects a very short encryption key (say 2 characters long), and another group selects a key with a more realistic length (over 6 characters long). A demo version of a commercial password breaking tool is then used to recover the keys with predictable results: the long one is impossible to retrieve within reasonable time.

2.3.3.7   Live System Analysis

The students were asked to collect as much data about a live system as possible in both the Windows and the Fedora Linux environments. This laboratory was not fully prescribed; the students were encouraged to explore options or commands not specifically mentioned in the instruction if they believed that such action would produce forensically interesting results.

The first part of the session used a set of free Windows tools created by Mark Russinovich and Bryce Cogswell, and available from Sysinternals Web [9]. To assure the soundness of the results the students were asked not to trust the cmd utility from the system being investigated, and to use the trusted command shell from the Helix Linux CD [28]. Sysinternals PsTools provide commands to list logged users, collect MAC times, list active processes, list executable files which opened the networks ports, and more. Additionally Helix provides the Windows Forensic Toolchest (WFT) [22] with more tools for collecting information about the system. Helix also offers the Investigator Notes module which allows storing date and time stamped notes on the external media, thus creating a proper forensically sound record of all activities.

In the second part of the session the workstations were booted in the Fedora Linux environment, and information was collected with the standard Linux commands. Thus the operating system and hardware specifications were collected with the command uname –a and uptime, MAC times were recorded with ls, active processes were listed with the ps aux command redirecting output to ps.txt file, and the powerful netstat command was used to determine open ports and associated applications. This demonstrated to the students that Linux without any additional computer forensics tools offers a powerful set of commands capable of collecting information about the system.

2.4   Commercial Software Alternative

We have considered whether it is necessary to give students access to commercial computer forensics software packages. It seems obvious that being able to work with a commercial package would enhance the general student experience, and provide opportunities for various certifications. The real question is whether it is strictly necessary in order to give the students a well rounded education. After reviewing the market we decided to take a balanced approach with the predominance of free open source software. We believe that it is of greater benefit to a student to be able to work from 'first principles', and to be able to conduct the investigation using simple tools like hex editors and command line utilities. Some exposure to dedicated software tools is also desirable, but only after the students learn to operate at the lower level of abstraction. All commercial distributors offer specific training courses for their products, and it is the usual practice for employers to finance such courses for their professional employees. The market changes continuously and it is not the goal of university education to give students specific skills with specific software products. Rather the students should be given sufficient foundation knowledge and learning skills to be able to gain the full benefit from commercial training if and when it is appropriate.

The computer forensic software companies are mostly small organisations, and typically they are not willing to grant free educational licences. One notable exception is ProDiscover [4], which offers a cut-down version of their software free of charge. This version was included in some of the laboratory exercises, mainly to demonstrate basic data carving techniques.

Another popular commercial package is the Forensic Toolkit (FTK) from AccessData. This software can be installed and used on any machine in evaluation mode, which restricts the number of files which can be analysed. The current limit is 5000 files, which makes it unsuitable for commercial work, but does not affect the educational application, as the test cases studied are limited in size. We demonstrated FTK to students in a lecture, and we intended to use it more extensively for laboratory work in this year's delivery of the Computer Forensics Workshop. Unfortunately commercial companies frequently change their policies regarding educational or free use of commercial software. Here are some examples:

- EnCase from Guidance Software [6] distributes sets of EnCase software and sample files which are intended to be used together. No other files will open in the demo version of Encase, thus preventing unlicensed use. While this approach is reasonable it requires following in the footsteps of Guidance Software prepared training cases and thus is restrictive.

- ProDiscover Basic from Technology Pathways [14] offers unrestricted use of their "Basic" version, so exercises can be tailored to specific needs. The only small concern is that this software has not been updated for some time now and thus it is not clear what its future is.
- Forensic Toolkit AccessData offered a free version limited to 5000 files which was suitable for educational purposes. Unfortunately the new release (FTK 2.0) can not be downloaded from AccessData any more, and at this stage it is unclear whether there is any support for free restricted use.

Other commercial vendors simply refuse to provide any free versions of their software for educational purpose, typically ignoring any inquiries. This is easy to understand within a mindset of commercial vendors: all of them in addition to selling software also offer various very expensive training courses (typically around US$ 1,000 per day) and thus, most likely, their marketing department considers universities as undesirable competition.

2.5   Conclusions and Future Work

Based on the feedback we received from our students and our peers, the computer forensics stream we designed and implemented thoroughly prepares students to begin their professional career in computer forensics, starting as assistants for experienced investigators and developing into fully-fledged computer forensics professionals serving both industry and law enforcement agencies. The currently available computer forensics open source software fulfilled most of the needs we had for the practical part of the delivery. The students completing the subject gained thorough knowledge of the forensic process, and would have no problem applying this knowledge using whatever tools are available. The Computer Forensics Workshop was also well received by practising computing professionals who enrolled as so called non-award students. Based on our experience and materials we collected, a similar subject is currently being introduced at the Warsaw University of Technology.

The body of knowledge in computer forensics, similarly to computer science – the discipline it emerged from – grows at a very rapid pace. It means that the specific content of the workshop will have to be constantly reviewed and adjusted. Our growing research strength in computer forensics also contributes to this process. We envisage that in future deliveries we will have to dedicate more space to memory forensics, live systems investigations as well as storage and systems virtualisation. With the continuing development of the open source forensics software products we will be able to develop laboratory work to match these changes. We intend to have a close look at an alternative Sleuthkit interface, PTK [15] with the view to include it in the future deliveries. PTK is currently in beta stage and promises to implement numerous new features essential for forensics investigations which should offer a great deal of features like analysis, search and management of complex cases, etc.

Another area which we would like to expand is the law content of the computer forensics stream. In particular it would be beneficial to the students who are likely to serve as expert witnesses to have practice in presenting evidence in a court of law. This kind of practice is useful to students in all forensic disciplines; it is not specific to computer forensics.

To summarise, the Computer Forensics Workshop was a demonstrable success. It is clear that it fulfilled students' expectations, and provided them with skills and knowledge that they will be able to apply in their professional life. This overall experience was enriched by the laboratory work based predominantly on FLOSS software products.

References

1. AccessData (2008). http://www.accessdata.com/. Accessed 2 March 2008
2. ACM Computing Curricula 2001 Computer Science (2001). http://www.computer.org/portal/cms_docs_ieeecs/ieeecs/education/cc2001/cc2001.pdf. Accessed 3 December 2006
3. BackTrack, Remote-Exploit.org. http://www.remote-exploit.org/backtrack.html. Accessed 1 August 2007
4. Computer Forensic Tool for Law Enforcement (2006). http://www.techpathways.com/ProDiscoverDFT.htm. Accessed 20 October 2006
5. DEFT (2008) http://deft.yourside.it/index.php. Accessed 18 February 2008
6. EnCase Forensic Modules (2007) http://www.guidancesoftware.com/products/ef_modules.asp. Accessed 17 December 2007
7. INSERT Inside Security Rescue Toolkit. http://www.inside-security.de/insert_en.html. Accessed 28 November 2007
8. Microsoft, Alternatives to the Directory Replicator Service (2006)
9. Microsoft, Windows Sysinternals (2007) http://www.microsoft.com/technet/sysinternals/default.mspx. Accessed 12 June 2007
10. Microsoft, Windows Research Kernel (2006) www.microsoft.com/WindowsAcademic. Accessed 15 November 2008
11. NTI (2008) http://www.forensics-intl.com/index.html. Accessed on 30 June 2007
12. Paraben Corporation (2008) http://www.paraben.com/. Accessed on 30 March 2008
13. Pasco(2008)http://sourceforge.net/project/shownotes.php?release_id=152387&group_id=78332. Accessed 21 June 2008
14. ProDiscover Forensics (2006) http://www.techpathways.com/ProDiscoverDFT.htm. Accessed 20 October 2006
15. PTK an alternative Sleuthkit interface - DFLabs (2008) http://ptk.dflabs.com/. Accessed 31 August 2008
16. The Open Group Base Specifications Issue 6 (2004) http://www.opengroup.org/onlinepubs/009695399/utilities/dd.html. Accessed 21 March 2007
17. True Crypt - Free Open-Source On-The-Fly Disk Encryption Software (2007) http://www.truecrypt.org/. Accessed 15 January 2007
18. University of Western Sydney Handbook (2008) http://handbook.uws.edu.au/hbook/course.asp?course=3506. Accessed 6 February 2008
19. University of Western Sydney Handbook – units (2008) http://handbook.uws.edu.au/hbook/unit.asp?unit=300447.1. Accessed 10 March 2008
20. VMware. http://www.vmware.com/. Accessed 10 March 2008
21. Web Historian http://www.download.com/Web-Historian/3000-2653_4-10373157.html?part=dl-RedCliffW&subj=dl&tag=button&cdlPid=10562519. Accessed 21 June 2008

22. Windows Forensic Toolchest (WFT) (2007) http://www.foolmoon.net/security/wft/. Accessed on 15 June 2008
23. Wireshark (2008) http://www.wireshark.org/about.html. Accessed 20 November 2007
24. X-Ways Software Technology AG (2007) http://www.winhex.com/. Accessed 7 October 2006
25. Xen. http://xen.org/. Accessed 9 June 2007
26. Bem D (2008) Open Source Virtual Environments in Computer Forensics, the 1st Workshop on Open Source Software for Computer and Network Forensics, Milan , Italy
27. Carrier B (2007) The Sleuth Kit. http://www.sleuthkit.org/sleuthkit/desc.php. Accessed 10 February 2007
28. E-fence, The HELIX Live CD (2007) http://www.e-fense.com/helix/. Accessed 9 Feb. 2007
29. Farmer D, Venema W (2007) The Coroner's Toolkit (TCT). http://www.porcupine.org/forensics/tct.html. Accessed 25 April 2007
30. Gottschalk L, Liu J, Dathan B, Fitzgerald S, Stein M (2005) Computer forensics programs in higher education: a preliminary study, SIGCSE Technical Symposium on Computer Science Education, 203–231
31. Grundy BJ (2007) The Law Enforcement and Forensic Examiner – Introduction to Linux – A Beginner's Guide to Linux as a Forensic Platform. http://www.linuxleo.com/Docs/linuxintro-LEFE-3.21.pdf. Accessed on 17 March 2008
32. Hentea M, Dhillon HS, Dhillon M (2006) Towards Changes in Information Security Education. Journal of Information Technology Education 5:221–233
33. Huebner E and Bem D (2008) Forensic Extraction of EFS Encrypted Files in Live System Investigation, Journal of Digital Forensic Practice 2:1–12
34. Russon R, Fledel Y (2004) NTFS Documentation, Free Software Foundation, Inc.
35. Yasinsac A, Erbacher RF, Marks DG, Pollitt MM, Sommer PM (2003), Computer Forensics Education. IEEE Security and Privacy 1(4):15–23

Chapter 3
Virtual Machine for Computer Forensics – the Open Source Perspective

Derek Bem

Abstract In this paper we discuss the potential role of virtual environments in the analysis phase of computer forensics investigations. We argue that commercial closed source computer forensics software has certain limitations, and we propose a method which may lead to gradual shift to open source software (OSS). A brief overview of virtual environments and open source software tools is presented and discussed. Further we identify current limitations of virtual environments leading to the conclusion that the method is very promising, but at this point in time it can not replace conventional techniques of computer forensics analysis. We demonstrate that using Virtual Machines (VM) in Linux environments can complement the conventional techniques, and often can bring faster and verifiable results not dependent on proprietary, close source tools.

3.1 Introduction

In our previous work [17] we examined possible roles virtual environments can play in the analysis phase of computer forensics investigations, and we identified the limitations of virtual environments. Our conclusion was that virtual environments at this stage can not be considered as a replacement of conventional techniques of computer evidence analysis. We continued our work [16] by demonstrating how virtual environments can be successfully used in the analysis phase of the computer forensics investigation of portable USB flash drives to complement conventional methods of computer evidence analysis. In this paper we go further by analysing open source and free virtualization tools and testing their suitability in various computer forensics applications.

D. Bem (✉)
Computer Forensis Consulting, 324 GWH, Warrimoo, NSW 2774, Australia
e-mail: dbem@computerforensis.com

E. Huebner and S. Zanero (eds.), *Open Source Software for Digital Forensics*,
DOI 10.1007/978-1-4419-5803-7_3, © Springer Science+Business Media, LLC 2010

We provide a brief overview of virtualisation and applications concentrating on open source software. We than consider suitability of virtual environments as a tool in computer forensics investigations, where virtualisation could be of use in two distinct areas:

- Recreating the investigated environment by booting the original system in a virtual environment. We argue that this application is of limited use because of a series of technical difficulties preventing full recreation of the original environment.
- Creating an environment where different operating systems coexist on the same hardware and have access to the same image being investigated.

We argue that the second option is the best application of virtualisation in the computer forensics field. Additionally we believe that it can lead to a gradual shift from closed source to open source tools and decrease reliance on expensive, proprietary software products.

3.2   Overview of Virtualisation Methods

Virtualization is a relatively old concept dating back to the early 1960s when the IBM Watson Research Center did a lot of groundbreaking work in this field leading to the first commercial products [22]. It is interesting to note that when this paper was written (late 2008) the IT job market was considered to be depressed with a low demand for specialists in most areas, however at the same time according to Datamation magazine "one IT sector seems unaffected by this flat trend: virtualization" [26]. Since the 1960s virtualisation became well established, but often poorly understood. In the broadest possible way virtualisation can be seen as the abstraction of computer resources. This is illustrated in Fig. 3.1 which shows one operating system (OS 4) which runs directly on available computer hardware resources, and three another operating systems (OS 1, OS 2 and OS 3) which run using virtual resources allocated to them by software. Each operating system can check what resources are allocated to it: what are CPU parameters, how much memory it has at its disposal, etc. Ideally the operating systems OS 1 – OS 3 (typically referred to as 'guests') are not aware that their resources are allocated differently than for the system OS 4. This is achieved in one of many different ways.

Major approaches are described below in relation to their suitability for computer forensics. It should be noted that any attempt to formally categorise software is very difficult, as each software product uses a mixed approach to optimise the end result, and rarely belongs to one category.

Table 3.1 lists some commercial, free and Open Source virtualisation products. The list does not pretend to be complete in any way. Our opinion as to suitability of each tool to computer forensics should be seen as approximation of our own experiences. The list serves to illustrate various solutions rather than to attempt a formal classification. The main approaches to virtualisation have many conceptual similarities (see Fig. 3.1); however sometimes there are also considerable differences.

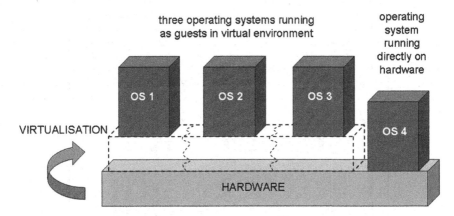

Fig. 3.1 Concept of resources virtualisation, host system and guest systems

Hardware Virtualization is probably the easiest concept to understand, but it is difficult to implement. In hardware virtualisation one or more virtual machines are created to fully emulate "real" hardware of the underlying computer. Standard, unmodified hardware is used, and there is no special hardware support for any virtualisation specific instructions. As all CPU instructions need to be emulated in software, hardware virtualisation performance is typically poor. The advantage is that the guest operating systems do not require any modifications.

Hardware Enabled Virtualisation is similar to the above, but it benefits from the architectural support of modern CPUs specially designed to make implementing the virtualisation easier. Most current Intel CPUs support Intel Virtualization Technology (known as IVT, VT or "Vanderpool") [21]. Similarly, most current AMD CPUs support AMD Virtualisation (known as AMD-V or "Pacifica") [1]. The CPU level support for virtualisation provides interrupt delivery to individual virtual machines, improves memory address translation removing the need for virtual machines to use Direct Memory Access (DMA), and provides other mechanisms. It is beyond the scope of this paper to analyse IVT and AMD-V, and curious reader is referred to comprehensive literature.

Full (or Native) Virtualisation relies on hypervisor (also known as virtual machine monitor) which is software located between hardware and virtual guests. Hypervisor role is to control the host processor and all resources, and to allocate them as required to each guest operating system. If this simulation of the underlying hardware is complete the virtual guest machines have the illusion of running on the same hardware as the hypervisor runs on. What follows is that an operating system which is installed in the virtual guest environment does not require any modification, and ideally it should not be aware that it runs in a virtual, not real, environment.

Paravirtualisation also uses the concept of hypervisor, but it differs from the native virtualisation by requiring modifications to the guest operating system. The guest is aware of running in a virtual environment, and it must be able to

Table 3.1 Some virtualisation software products and their suitability in computer forensics application

Software	Type	Developer, major distributions	Licence	computer forensics suitability
Bosch	emulation	Mandriva	GNU LGPL	poor to average
KVM	full virtualisation	included in Linux kernel since 2.6.20	GNU LGPL	used by QUEMU, VirtualBox, Xen
Linux-VServer	patching Linux kernel to add operating system-level virtualisation	many	GNU LGPL	poor
OpenVZ	operating system-level virtualisation	OpenVZ project is supported by Parallels	GNU LGPL	poor to average
Solaris Containers	operating system-level virtualisation	Sun, Solaris, OpenSolaris	CDDL	good
Sun xVM, OpenxVM	family of virtualisation products	Sun Microsystems	varies, some GNU GPL	good to very good
QEMU	processor emulator	Fabrice Bellard. Many	GNU LGPL	see Xen and VirtualBox
Virtual PC	emulation	Microsoft (written by Connectix)	free	average to good
VirtualBox	full virtualisation	innotek GmbH, now Sun. Many	GNU LGPL	good to very good
VMWare	full virtualisation	VMWare	proprietary, some free (server)	good to very good
Xen	para virtualisation and HVM (hardware virtual machine)	University of Cambridge	commercial: Citrix Systems, some GPL	Good to very good
z/VM	full virtualisation	IBM. Longest tradition of VM products	proprietary	? requires IBM z/Architecture hardware

handle a set of special hypercalls originating in the hypervisor. As a result the virtual guest operating system is aware that it runs on hardware which is not identical to that of the underlying computer.

Operating System Level Virtualization does not introduce any additional layers between the host and the guests. The host itself is suitably created or modified to support virtual guests, and all the guests share the same host environment. Similarly to hardware and full virtualisations the guests do not require any modifications.

It should be noted that some virtual environment software can run on computers with or without additional hardware virtualisation support at the CPU instruction level. Sometimes it may be difficult to classify which of the above groups a specific software product belongs to and it may fit in more than one area.

3.3 Virtual Environments in Computer Forensics Investigations

According to one of the earliest definitions offered in 1999 by the Australian Institute of Criminology [27] computer forensics is "the process of identifying, preserving, analysing and presenting digital evidence in a manner that is legally acceptable". A bit later the U.S. Department of Justice digital evidence guide [25] formalised the important step of the process, advising to: "Acquire the subject evidence to the examiner's storage device using the appropriate software and hardware tools". 'Acquire the evidence' is still understood by many investigators as making a physical copy of computer storage, typically performing a disk-to-disk copy, usually using the Unix / Linux dd based utility.

As computer technology develops it facilitates processing larger and larger volumes of data, which is not only transient but also not limited to any specific location, or a single storage media (like a single hard disk). Even in simple cases it is misleading to treat the hard disk storing data as synonymous with that data. Computer systems are increasingly complex, and analysing their parts, like the disk or memory image, may not readily reveal all available information. This calls for a new approach (one that is likely to remove the expectation of certainty) i.e. to attempt to recreate the computer system and its immediate environment by reproducing the collected images in a controlled way, and observe its behaviour. This has the potential to provide a valuable insight into the dynamic relationship of the investigated system with the outside computer networks, as well as the specific setups and functions of the system itself. The evidence obtained this way is not a physical object, like a hard disk, but resembles more a visit to the crime scene. The advantage is that this process can be repeated any number of times without any further damage to the evidence already collected.

The approach relying on copying a storage device is becoming increasingly difficult to implement and often impractical [20]. In our recent paper [15] we proposed to expand the computer forensics definition to include collection of hardware and software details of the investigated computer system with the aim to recreate the environment being investigated as closely and as fully as possible. We argue that it has to be accepted that it is not possible to copy the computing environment completely, nor to recreate it later in a completely faithful way. Many of those new challenges can be better addressed by skilful and appropriate use of virtualisation as well as better and wider use of open source software.

In Table 1 we listed some virtualisation software products and their suitability in computer forensics applications. The table shows only the selected products we used in our experiments over the last few years. The "computer forensics suitability" is our somewhat subjective assessment of the product and should not be seen as the result of thorough tests or applying formal criteria.

Bochs [2] is a hardware emulator and offers a very limited list of emulated devices. Most work is done by one developer only, however the product is stable and well maintained. Bochs is capable of running a good range of operating systems as guests, but because of the nature of emulations which relies on translating instructions performance is poor, and guests run very slowly. Mandriva [5] distribution includes Bochs on their live CD which makes it easy to try, however poor guest hardware support and poor performance make it at best only an average choice for computer forensics investigator.

Virtual PC [7], originally written by Connectix and subsequently acquired by Microsoft, is offered as a free software. It is a more mature product and emulates guest environments more efficiently, thus providing faster operation. However the problems mentioned above remain. Additionally, the suitability of current Virtual PC 2007 is further diminished for a computer forensics investigator by the fact that it can only run on Windows host and provides support for Windows guests only. While Linux or DOS guests can be run under Virtual PC this is not recommended and not officially supported. Because of good performance, stability and excellent guest – host integration we consider Virtual PC suitability for computer forensics application to be average to good.

Linux-VServer [4], OpenVZ [10] and Solaris Containers [11] add operating system-level virtualisation capabilities to the Linux kernel. Linux-VServer is not as actively developed as OpenVZ and Solaris Containers. We consider Open VZ to be slightly more suitable for a computer forensics investigator, as it offers very high (close to native) guest performance. Unfortunately both host and guest have to be Linux operating systems. Solaris Containers and Solaris Zones are part of Sun xVM family of virtualisation products, which really requires separate analysis beyond the scope of this paper. Sun virtualisation products are part of Sun Solaris distribution and offer excellent stability with very good hardware support and performance. Sun environment is a bit different, and from a forensic investigator perspective it may require a more dedicated and time consuming approach to use it, however stability, flexibility and good integration of the Sun virtualisation products is very promising.

Kernel-based Virtual Machine (KVM) [3] is full virtualisation currently implemented as a loadable kernel module for the x86 hardware installation. It also supports

Intel VT and AMD-V CPU virtualisation extensions. KVM is used by other virtualisations via the /dev/kvm interface to set up the guests. Some of these products are QEMU, VirtualBox and Xen. We found VirtualBox and Xen to be particularly stable, well documented and easy to use as described later in this paper in more details.

Finally the list would not be complete without mentioning VMWare products [13]. Apart from IBM (not covered here) and Sun Microsystems VMWare is one of the largest companies involved in virtualisation and offers a wide range of commercial products. VMWare Server is offered free for Windows and Linux platforms, it is very well documented, easy to use. Unfortunately some advanced features such as managing multi-tier configurations and multiple snapshots, which would be of interest to a computer forensics investigator are not available in VMware Server and are offered only in a commercially sold Workstation version.

We evaluate below two main areas where virtualisation can be used in computer forensics application:

- (3.1) full recreation of investigated computer system in virtual environment, booting the acquired image as guest,
- (3.2) investigation of an acquired image in environment where different operating systems coexist on the same hardware.

Advantages and limitations of both are considered with particular focus on benefits flowing from skilful use Open Source tools and environment.

3.3.1 Booting Acquired Disk Image in Virtual Environment to Recreate Investigated Computer

During the process of the evidence acquisition typically a full bit by bit image of the investigated system is made using dd, a derivative of dd, or a functionally similar tool. If the imaged disk contains a full operating system the obvious investigative approach would be to copy it, preserve the original, and attempt to boot the copy. If the copy could be booted the investigator would be able to see the same environment as the original system when it was acquired. There are two possible approaches: copy the image to a similar, preferably identical storage media, and boot it on identical hardware. The other possible approach is to boot the image as a guest under virtual machine. Unfortunately while conceptually simple, both approaches are rather difficult to implement. We will consider a case when the original machine being investigated runs Windows operating system, simply because computers being investigated usually have such systems installed, and to demonstrate that open source tools are universally applicable.

The first approach, booting the acquired image to a new storage media, works well providing the image is rebuilt on identical hardware as the original machine. If the hardware is different we need to consider how Windows operating system reacts to the fact that the underlying hardware has changed. Older Windows coped with such hardware changes reasonably well, but current Windows Vista, XP and Server 2008 are affected by recently introduced Microsoft Product Activation policy [24], and do not cope with such hardware change very well.

During the product activation Windows checks ten areas of the computer and creates eight byte long hash number corresponding to the configuration. The check is selective, i.e. it uses only part of the CPU serial number, IDE and SCSI adapters, 'dockable' flag, BIOS ID, etc. The resulting eight bytes hardware hash value and Windows serial number are used by Microsoft to activate Windows, and is also verified on each login; if the hardware is detected as "substantially different", reactivation is required. The precise algorithm used to determine when the hardware is "substantially" different as opposed to "the same or similar" is not published by Microsoft for obvious reasons. Subsequently, when a full system is moved to different hardware for computer investigations a computer forensics technician can not be certain what will happen when the boot of the system is attempted: Windows may or may not request reactivation.

The most reliable approach would be to rebuild the acquired image on another hard disk using the Linux dd command, install it on the same PC from which it was acquired in the first place, and boot the system. This method is forensically sound, as no information is left on the powered off computer with its hard disk drive removed. Such an approach avoids another issue: windows detecting new devices when it is booted on different underlying hardware, and requesting installation of required device drivers. If new drivers are installed it can be argued that some parts of the system were changed, and depending on the specific scenario, this could possibly invalidate forensic findings. Unfortunately the original computer is often not available and thus can not be used.

The second approach, booting the acquired image as a guest under virtual machine is more promising from the forensics point of view; however it is still affected by limitations imposed by Microsoft Product Activation mechanism. Guest virtual machines offer a very limited range of emulated hardware, for example just one video adapter, one standard IDE hard disk controller, etc. We ran a series of tests using different virtual machines, including commercial VMWare server with disappointing results. While some combinations of virtualisation software run on Linux host allowed for the acquired Windows XP and Vista image to boot as a guest, Windows always detected virtual hardware as being "substantially different", and requested reactivation. Another issue we faced was that time differences between the booted image and virtual environment was interpreted by the Windows guest as attempt to boot over 30 days after the original activation, and the system was shut down. We were not successful in attempts to overcome this problem by setting back the virtual machine clock, though this is one area worth investigating.

There are two possible solutions to the above problem, though each one of them has serious disadvantages:

- to provide virtual machine support for as many hardware devices as are supported under Windows. This is unrealistic, as it would require enormous effort from many people only to satisfy one possible application of virtual machines.

- to pass information to Windows that it runs on already activated hardware, even if it is not the same as the original configuration.

The second solution (simulating "Windows already activated" condition) is relatively easy to implement, but it would most likely be seen by Microsoft as software piracy. It is based on a weakness of Microsoft Product Activation method, which provides an option of so called "OEM Activation" or "OA". OA allows properly licensed Original Equipment Manufacturer (OEM) to include Windows activation code in their BIOS [6], and any future hardware changes do not trigger the request to reactivate the system, as long as the BIOS is recognised as licensed. The mechanism was improved from the original OA 1.0 to OA 2.0, but it is still open to abuse, and Microsoft is fully aware of that [8]. It is relatively easy to write a piece of software which intercepts all Windows BIOS checking commands, and returns information that the underlying hardware is OA enabled. If such BIOS emulator software would be included as part of virtualisation, the issue of reactivation of a guest operating system could be removed. Unfortunately most likely Microsoft would not allow for such an emulator to be included as part of virtualisation.

3.2 Accessing Disk Images From Different Operating Systems

Accessing disk images from different operating systems is more promising than the previously described approach. The idea is to create a setup which offers a wider range of tools and a more powerful open source based environment to investigate the acquired image. The following main steps are suggested:

- selected, stable distribution of Linux is installed as host, and preferred virtual machine is installed on the host,
- Windows XP or Vista (or both) are installed as a guest operating system(s),
- the acquired image is mounted on the host Linux.

The environment described above has a series of advantages over the approach which is currently common, specifically:

Less reliance on closed source software: typically Windows environment is used to investigate acquired images, and most tools are Windows based. The proposed setup does not require any drastic change in this approach, but introduces a parallel, Linux based environment and tools which an investigator may use to check or complement the findings obtained from Windows tools.

Cost savings: most software tools currently used in computer forensics investigations are created for Windows platform, are closed, proprietary solutions, and are very expensive. It is not unusual for a single software package to cost US$5,000 or more with a strict limit of licensing one copy per one machine. By contrast open source tools are obviously free.

Skill expansion: many skilled investigators were trained in Windows environment and have little reason to change to open source systems. However if they are offered a dual environment which is as easy to use as Windows environment they are comfortable with, they will start using tools from both, and soon will find advantages of open source software. As a result they will be ready to analyse Linux systems when the need arises.

Verification of findings: many researchers stress this as a very important advantage of open source tools [19], [18]. It is clear that when using close source tools one can not completely prove what was done, and to what extent the procedure used was forensically nonintrusive, or that the original files were not affected. While in most investigations such proof may not be required, in critical cases being unable to demonstrate a full understanding of the tool may lead to challenging the validity of the findings.

Verification of tools: access to full code allows for verifying behaviours of the tool. Again, this is typically not required, but in critical investigations it may be of crucial importance.

3.3.3 Shifting of Computer Forensics Environment From Windows to Linux

We believe that the main advantage of the environment proposed above is creating a mechanism for natural migration from Windows environment and tools to Linux platform.

There were many attempts to show the advantages of using Linux tools to analyse not only Linux, but also Windows images [23], [24]. Unfortunately it would require a bold and most likely unpopular decision within a computer forensics investigative organisation to change from Windows to Linux environment. The proposed method of using virtual machine environment has the unique advantage of "not burning bridges": every investigator working in Linux host environment with Windows running as a guest would still have full access to the familiar Windows set of tools. Moreover such investigator is not forced to use any environment in preference to another, they are left to discover the advantages of new tools without any pressure to do so. The same disk image which is analysed from Windows guest with Windows based tools is at the same time mounted on Linux host and can be accessed with native Linux tools. It is natural that an investigator in such parallel Windows/Linux environment would start trying Linux tools, and benefit from new and powerful utilities as well as techniques not available under Windows.

3.4 openSUSE And Other Linux Distributions

There are many stable Linux distributions which are suitable as hosts for forensic virtual application. We used openSUSE, Ubuntu, Fedora, Mandriva, Debian and a few other. It is difficult to say which one is most suitable for Linux computer forensic platform; many distributions are excellent. In most of our tests we used openSUSE [6]. We believe that close cooperation between Novell and the openSUSE community program resulted in a very well supported, stable and frequently updated distribution. Additionally openSUSE includes a set of mature virtual software packages of interest to a forensic instigator: Xen, VirtualBox, QEMU and KVM.

OpenSUSE (and SUSE) features user friendly setup and configuration tool YaST (Yet another Setup Tool). This allows an investigator familiar with Windows environment to activate and control the virtual guest operating system setup with the user friendly interface. There are many other properties of openSUSE which in our opinion make it one of the best choices for computer forensics virtualisation. We already listed some of main virtualisation products with our brief opinion of their suitability in computer forensics investigations. We will now describe in more details use of two such products which we found particularly interesting: VirtualBox and Xen.

3.4.1 openSUSE and VirtualBox

Sun xVM VirtualBox [8] (originally developed by innotek GmbH – spelled with small "i") comes as a standard package with openSuse. Of special significance to people coming from Windows environment is VirtualBox, which offers a powerful yet friendly user interface (see Fig. 3.2) and excellent documentation.

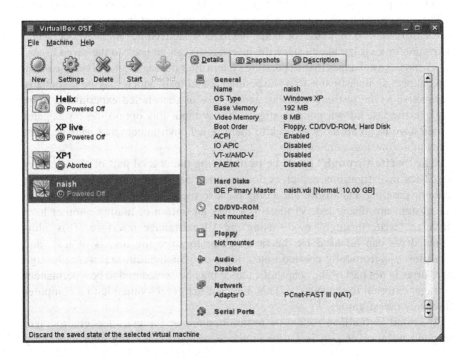

Fig. 3.2 VirtualBox running on openSUSE

VirtualBox supports a large selection of guests, including all recent versions of Windows, with some limited support for older environments (DOS, Windows 3.x / 95 / 98 / ME). Creating a new guest operating system is wizard guided, thus it does not require an in depth knowledge of Linux. The guest operating system parameters can also be changed from the control panel, which allows for fine tuning the amount of RAM, fixed or expanding size for virtual disk, and other configuration parameters.

There are many properties of VirtualBox which are of particular interest to a computer forensics investigator. The investigator has full control over which CD, DVD or floppy mounted on the host should be also accessible from the virtual guest environment. Of special value to forensics are options of **cloning**, **saving** the state of the machine, the **snapshots** and **"write-through" mode.**

Cloning allows duplicating hard disk image files on the same host to produce a second virtual machine with the same setup. This allows an investigator to try various tools with no fear of damaging the evidence, as at any time they can discard the corrupted image, go back and use the previously cloned one. The process of cloning is fast and easy to initiate.

Saving the machine state is an option offered at powering the guest off: if selected, the virtual machine state freezes, and saves its state to the hard disk. When the virtual machine is rebooted it continues from the state it was stopped at. This allows a investigator to stop the experiments and tests, power off the guest environment, and later power it on and continue. It is similar to the suspend option in laptop computers.

The snapshot allows saving the current state of a virtual machine at any time without powering it off. If tests and experiments performed in the virtual machine guest turn out to be of no use, or damaging to the system (for example by accidental activation of a virus), at any stage the investigator can go back to the saved "snapshot" state. Any changes to the operating system after the snapshot will be discarded. This allows an investigator to try experiments and tests which may be potentially destructive to the test environment, and in case of such failed experiments to go back to the last known good configuration. Without this option the investigator would have to go all the way back to the original environment and recreate other steps in a slow, less efficient way.

The "write-through" mode helps managing the crucial part of all computer forensics investigations, which is documenting all steps. In case of saving the state or creating a snapshot and going back to the previous state all changes to the system are discarded. VirtualBox offers an option of adding another hard drive in "write-through" mode using the VBoxManage interface. This additional drive can be used by the investigator to store the results of tests and analyses, electronically created notes, logs, etc. Such additional write-through hard drive is not part of the snapshots, thus it may be considered to be a permanent storage, external to the system. This makes it extremely valuable to a computer forensics investigator.

We rated VirtualBox suitability to build computer forensics test environment as good because of polished user interface, support for many guest operating systems, ability to freeze the system and to create snapshots, and easy control over host storage and virtualised storage.

3.4.2   openSUSE and Xen

Xen [14] is an open source paravirtualising virtual machine monitor (VMM), or hypervisor for the x86 processor architecture. Xen differes from the older IBM VM/370, and current VMWare and VirtualPC by requiring some modification to the host kernel. Guest operating systems run on Xen modified host with close-to-native performance. Xen supports both paravirtualisation and full virtualisation, and can use modern processor virtualisation technologies: Intel VT or AMD-V.

From the user perspective Xen is stable and offers high performance. OpenSUSE YaST2 Control Center makes it very easy to install the hypervisor and the tools, and to add and manage virtual machines, see Fig. 3.3. It is also as well documented as VirtualBox, possibly even better as there are five books in print dedicated to Xen.

Xen system uses multiple layers, starting from Xen itself which is referred to as "Domain 0" or "Dom0". Xen runs a process named xend which manages guests, named "Domain U" or "DomU". Xen (Dom0) kernel runs in processor Ring 0, which is the most privileged level interacting directly with the physical hardware. The hosted domains (or guests) run in Ring 1, while the unmodified applications run in Ring 3.

Computer architecture concepts of four privilege levels (or rings), and the associated terminology are not likely to be well understood by an average computer forensics investigator, but when using Xen this knowledge is not necessary; Xen provides full management access using an easy to understand graphics interface. Virtual machine creation is guided by a series of wizards, see Fig. 3.3, and can be controlled from Virtual Machine manager, see Fig. 3.4. This makes it possible, even easy for a computer forensics investigator with little Linux knowledge to control the whole environment.

Xen offers many options which are of interest to a computer forensics investigator. Two of them are: **Standard and Live Migration of Virtual Machines**. Standard Migration allows transferring a domain between two physical computers, but Live Migration is unique: it allows migrating the virtual machine between computers when the domain is running. During the process of live migration the full virtual machine including memory is transferred to another host. This opens new possibilities for a team of computer forensics investigators to better and more efficiently handle complex cases when different expertise may be required to analyse various scenarios or various aspects of the acquired image. In a conventional environment such tasks would be achieved by the slower and more error prone approach of duplicating environments and recreating them on another investigator's workstation.

Similarly to VirtualBox, Xen allows the investigator to control which CD, DVD or floppy mounted on the host should be also accessible from the virtual guest

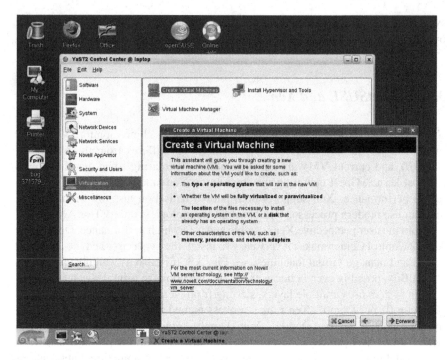

Fig. 3.3 Creating Xen Virtual Machine

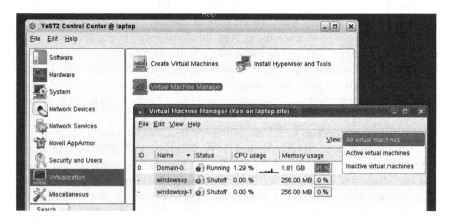

Fig. 3.4 Managing Xen Virtual Machines

environment. Fig. 3.5 shows openSUSE desktop with a virtual machine guest running Windows XP, with the fragment enlarged for clarity on Fig. 3.6. Note that Xen allows for a disk or a disk image to be mounted and equally accessible from the host operating system (in this case openSUSE) and from the guest operating system

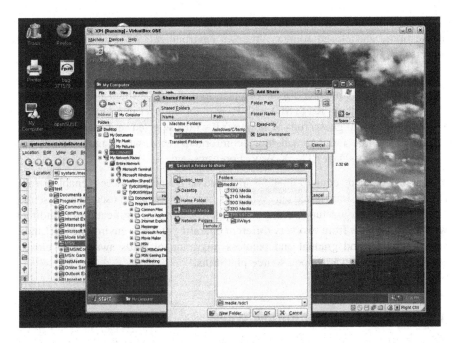

Fig. 3.5 Sharing folders and images between host and guest (see Figure 3.6 for enlarged section)

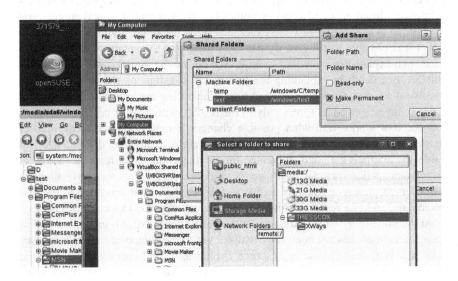

Fig. 3.6 Sharing folders and images between host and guest, enlarged section

(in this case Windows XP). This allows the investigator to use preferred tools on any platform, and apply them to the same image.

The investigator also has the option to selectively add folders to be shared between the guest and the host systems (see Fig. 6), and if required, to make them read-only to prevent any changes to the original files.

Xen has terrific potential in bridging the gap between open source platforms and applications, and closed source Windows environment. An example of a very powerful computer forensics environment is as follows:

- Dom0 (host) runs on any preferred Linux platform with standard Linux utilities and additional computer forensics open source tools, which may include for example The Sleuth Kit (TSK) with PTK graphical user interface,
- DomU (a virtual guest) runs Windows XP with a selected set of tools the investigator is more familiar and more comfortable with, which may include for example AccessData FTK, X-Ways Forensics, etc.

The investigated acquired image is mounted on Dom0 with access enabled from DomU, and both Linux based and Windows based tools can be used to analyse the same image. Such a setup has the advantage of allowing verification of findings with different tools from two very different operating systems environments (Linux and Windows), and gradual and painless migration of skills away from closed source platforms towards open source platforms.

3.5 Conclusions and Future Work

We believe that using free and open source software to build a computer forensics setup with virtual host and guest machines has great potential in making analysis of acquired evidentiary data more exact, and often faster. An additional advantage is that it is possible to fully verify the tools used, and to explain what they really do, if such explanation is needed or requested during the formal court proceedings. This level of depth in explaining the process of investigating the evidence is not possible if a software tool is closed source. When using commercial, closed source tools, an investigator has access only to the results, with little or no explanation of how the tool works, and what possible changes it may introduce to the master image being looked at. While commercial tools are typically well documented and stable, the internals are not documented for obvious commercial reasons. In critical cases when small errors can invalidate the evidence the findings may be challenged if the person presenting them is unable to fully explain what was done to the collected data, and as a result the findings may be inadmissible in a court of law.

At the same time our experiments have clearly shown that this great potential of open source tools has not been fully realised yet. For a computer forensics investigator who is planning to use open source virtualisation on Linux platform there are many options, but no clear guidelines and often no clear answer. In our future work we would like to more thoroughly investigate various Linux platforms and provide a more solid answer to question which one is the most suitable for computer forensics virtualisation. It is also unclear which method of virtualisation is best suitable for a specific task. While we had very encouraging results with both Xen and VirtualBox this is not to say that other virtualisation methods are less suitable. Possibly different methods could be recommended depending on the specific class of tasks.

Xen, VirtualBox and similar tools offer unprecedented power to tailor a computer forensics environment for complex investigations, including workgroups of investigators working from different locations on the same problem, and exchanging their full environments over the networks with minimal delay. This however requires more work to demonstrate complete, working examples and to encourage more research and practical work in developing a systematic approach.

Finally there are many Linux distributions aimed at forensics investigations: Helix, DEFT, SMART, Farmer's Boot CD (FBCD) to name only some. We intend to investigate the feasibility of creating a live CD Linux distribution which would include virtualisation tools aimed at a computer forensics investigator.

References

1. AMD (2008) AMD Industry Leading Virtualization Platform Efficiency http://www.amd.com/us-en/Processors/ProductInformation/0,,30_118_8796_14287,00.html Accessed 10 November 2007
2. Bochs IA-32 Emulator (2007) http://bochs.sourceforge.net/. Accessed 12 January 2008
3. Kernel Based Virtual Machine (2008) http://kvm.qumranet.com/kvmwiki/Front_Page. Accessed 22 January 2008
4. Linux-VServer (2008) http://linux-vserver.org/Welcome_to_Linux-VServer.org. Accessed on 30 January 2008
5. Mandriva (2008) http://www.mandriva.com/. Accessed 12 February 2008
6. Microsoft (2007) Microsoft Product Activation for Windows Vista® and Windows Server® 2008 (2008)
7. Microsoft (2007) Microsoft Virtual PC 2007 (2007) http://www.microsoft.com/windows/products/winfamily/virtualpc/default.mspx. Accessed 23 August 2007
8. Microsoft (2007) Microsoft Windows Genuine Advantage, Reported OEM BIOS Hacks http://blogs.msdn.com/wga/archive/2007/04/10/reported-oem-bios-hacks.aspx. Accessed 12 March 2008
9. openSUSE (2008) http://www.opensuse.org/. Accessed 2 February 2008
10. OpenVZ (2008) http://openvz.org/. Accessed 16 January 2008
11. Sun Microsystems Virtualization (2008) http://www.sun.com/software/solaris/virtualization.jsp. Accessed 1 March 2008
12. Sun xVM VirtualBox (2008) http://www.sun.com/software/products/virtualbox/index.jsp. Accessed 4 April 2008
13. VMWare (2007) http://www.vmware.com/. Accessed 22 November 2007
14. Xen (2008) http://xen.org/. Accessed 15 February 2008
15. Bem D, Feld F, Huebner E et al (2008) Computer Forensics – Past, Present and Future. Journal of Information Science and Technology, Volume 5 Issue 3
16. Bem D, Huebner E (2007) Analysis of USB Flash Drives in a Virtual Environment. Small Scale Digital Device Forensic Journal, Volume 1 Issue 1
17. Bem D, Huebner E (2007) Computer Forensics Analysis in Virtual Environments. International Journal of Digital Evidence, Volume 6 Issue 2
18. Carrier B (2005) File System Forensic Analysis. Addison-Wesley, Upper Saddle River
19. Carrier B (2007) The Sleuth Kit. http://www.sleuthkit.org/sleuthkit/desc.php. Accessed 1 February 2007
20. Carvey H (2007) Windows Forensic Analysis. Syngress, Rockland
21. Chao L (2006) Intel Virtualization Technology. Intel Technology Journal, doi: 10.1535/itj.1003

22. DuCharme B (1994) The Operating Systems Handbook. McGraw-Hill Companies, New York
23. Farmer D, Venema W (2005) Forensic Discovery. Addison-Wesley, Upper Saddle River
24. Grundy BJ (2008) The Law Enforcement and Forensic Examiner's Introduction to Linux, A Beginner's Guide. http://www.linuxleo.com/Docs/linuxintro-LEFE-3.65.pdf. Accessed on 17 September 2008
25. Hart SV (2004) Forensic Examination of Digital Evidence: A Guide for Law Enforcement. www.ncjrs.gov/pdffiles1/nij/199408.pdf. Accessed on 7 March 2007
26. Maguire J (2008) Hottest IT Job Market: Virtualization. Datamation. http://itmanagement.earthweb.com/career/article.php/3746776/Hottest+IT+Job+Market:+Virtualization.htm. Accessed on 17 June 2008
27. McKemmish R (1999) What is Forensic Computing? Trends & Issues in Crime And Criminal Justice, Australian Institute of Criminology

Part II
Novel FLOSS Tools for Computer Forensics

Chapter 4
Open Computer Forensic Architecture a Way to Process Terabytes of Forensic Disk Images

Oscar Vermaas, Joep Simons, and Rob Meijer

Abstract This chapter describes the Open Computer Forensics Architecture (OCFA), an automated system that dissects complex file types, extracts metadata from files and ultimately creates indexes on forensic images of seized computers. It consists of a set of collaborating processes, called modules. Each module is specialized in processing a certain file type. When it receives a so called 'evidence', the information that has been extracted so far about the file together with the actual data, it either adds new information about the file or uses the file to derive a new 'evidence'. All evidence, original and derived, is sent to a router after being processed by a particular module. The router decides which module should process the evidence next, based upon the metadata associated with the evidence. Thus the OCFA system can recursively process images until from every compound file the embedded files, if any, are extracted, all information that the system can derive, has been derived and all extracted text is indexed. Compound files include, but are not limited to, archive- and zip-files, disk images, text documents of various formats and, for example, mailboxes. The output of an OCFA run is a repository full of derived files, a database containing all extracted information about the files and an index which can be used when searching. This is presented in a web interface. Moreover, processed data is easily fed to third party software for further analysis or to be used in data mining or text mining-tools. The main advantages of the OCFA system are:

1. Scalability, it is able to process large amounts of data.
2. Extendable, it is easy to develop and plug in custom modules.
3. Open, the output is well suited to be used as input for other systems.
4. Analysts and tactical investigators may search the evidence without the constant intervention of digital investigators.

O. Vermaas (✉), J. Simons, and R. Meijer
KLPD, P.O. Box 100, 3970 AC Driebergen, the Netherlands
e-mails: oscar.vermaas@klpd.politie.nl; joep.simons@klpd.politie.nl; rob.meijer@klpd.politie.nl

E. Huebner and S. Zanero (eds.), *Open Source Software for Digital Forensics*,
DOI 10.1007/978-1-4419-5803-7_4, © Springer Science+Business Media, LLC 2010

4.1 Introduction

In the last years, the role of digital forensics in crime investigations has grown substantial and is still increasing. Not only the number of cases which involve digital forensics is growing, but also the size of the seized evidence is growing exponentially. The processing of evidence involves the following steps:

Gather data. Normally, a digital investigation starts with creating an image of a harddisk of some sort. This could be in its own right already be a challenge, and is a specialists task. The investigator has to take into account the possibilities of the hardware. However, this step is not covered by OCFA.

Unlock file systems. The investigator needs to identify partitions and on those partitions file systems need to be identified. These file systems may be regular file systems like NTFS, FAT, ext2 or ReiserFS, but can also be less well-known partition types like a raw partition used by Sybase. After the file system has been determined, the investigator recovers deleted files and retrieves regular files. The tasks just described are handled well by forensic toolkits such as Encase and FTK. In the open source community the Sleuthkit is well known for its capabilities in analyzing disk images.

Unlock files. The files found in the previous stage are processed further. This part consists of the following actions:

Filter unwanted files. For example there is no need to look at untampered windows system files. They can be removed by using a hash database.

Check for wanted files. This action also checks hashes against a database. However, in this case the presence of a file indicates something, for example, a database consisting of hashes of known stego tools.

Dissect archive files. These actions extract files from known archive types, for instance, outlook's pst' format, or zip files.

Convert files to an easy to read format. This action converts files that can only be read with specialized viewers, to a standardized format, usually plain text, so that it can be used in later processing.

Automatic analysis. Analyses that can be done automatically are e.g., the creation of indexes and timelines, some forms of text mining and the determination of OS type and user profile.

Finding Evidence. This part consists of the actual 'case investigation' work. Evidence might mean the existence of a file, the contents of a file or the relation between files over different systems. It does need an investigator with case knowledge.

A clear distinction exists between tactical and digital investigators in the Netherlands, as shown in Fig. 4.1. The job of the digital investigator is to facilitate access to the seized data. The digital investigator does not need to know about the contents of the seized evidence. There are many cases in which it is obvious that the digital investigator should only be concerned with providing access to the evidence. For instance, in a child abuse case, the digital investigator recovers multimedia files and hands them over to a vice detective. The vice detective classifies the pictures and determines whether they contain illegal content.

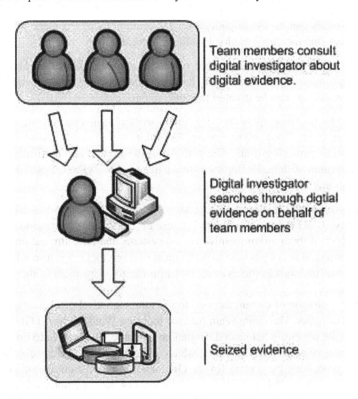

Team members consult digital investigator about digital evidence.

Digital investigator searches through digtial evidence on behalf of team members

Seized evidence

Fig. 4.1 Old way of interacting between a digital and a tactical investigator

One of the main tasks in digital investigations is to order information in such a way that it is easily accessible by tactical investigators. Normally this means that tactical investigators or analysts have to consult the digital investigator. In a large case this could be several investigators at the same time consulting the digital investigator, asking possibly redundant questions.

Although forensic tools already exist, some recent trends have aggravated the following problems, creating the need for something like OCFA.

- It is nowadays not uncommon to find terabytes of data in relatively small cases. Unfortunately, the given amount of time which is set by the law to complete certain phases in an investigation does not grow with the amount of data seized.
- Criminals not only use their machines to run their businesses, but also to communicate with each other. First of all, this means that more specialized analysts like accountants are getting involved in investigating seized digital evidence. Secondly, sophisticated analysis of data and cross analysis of seized evidence is becoming important to expose these criminal organizations.
- The diversity of data increases at both the file system level, in the form of different file systems, and in the amount of different file format. It is no longer reasonable that one tool supports all.
- Computer investigations are getting more complex. It is not feasible for an untrained person to do a computer investigation. Only highly trained IT

professionals can do investigations for large amounts of PC's and/or complex networks. This increases the load on digital investigators.

From the above it is obvious that techniques are needed to prepare seized evidence automatically so that non-digital investigators can access it easily.

Current solutions can be divided into two categories:

- Forensic tools. These tools are specifically written to investigate one comprise, in random order, Ilook, FTK, Encase, Sleuthkit.
- Information gathering tools. These tools are written to automatically analyze large amounts of data. Examples in this category are ZyFind, Spss Clementine or Autonomy.

These tools however all have some shortcomings. First, none has all required functionality. This becomes a problem because of lack of tool integration across all vendors. Most of them are monolithic closed systems and have limited import- and export functions. It is not possible to script most of those tools. It is also not possible to add certain functions to the existing tool in order to adapt them to the particular need of a case.

Another limitation of current forensic tools is the high level of interaction needed with the investigator. The mainstream forensic tools are Windows based GUI applications which are not easily automated. Digital investigators do not want to find an error message dialogue on Monday morning, which was generated on Friday evening stalling further processing by waiting for the OK button to be pressed. Especially in big cases, one wants to be able to process large amounts of data as automated batch jobs.

Finally, most of the interfaces in the forensic tools are very complex and different. Although this gives a lot of power to the investigator, it also requires a lot of specialized knowledge. This is not desirable for the tactical investigator.

4.1.1 Problem Statement

From the above it is clear that functionality is lacking from current digital forensic tools. To solve this problem the Research and Development Team of the Team Digital Expertise of the Dutch National Police Agency[1] started the development of OCFA. The aim was to develop a tool that can rapidly and automatically unlock file systems and files and, if possible, do some automatic analysis.

In addition to the above, the system must meat the following boundary conditions:

- Preserving Chain of Evidence. It should always be clear and reproducable how a file was derived from the original image.
- Openness. The derived evidence and features must be accessible to other applications and users, e.g. image viewers or text mining tools.
- Scalability. The design must allow to upscale components to keep pace with growing workloads.

---

[1] The official Dutch name is Korps landelijke politiediensten (KLPD).

- Stability. The system must at least be in a recoverable state when a component stops for some reason.
- Modularity. Because of the growing amount of different file systems and file formats, it should be possible to easily extend the system.
- Ease of use. A tactical investigator, with little digital expertise, should be able to use the GUI.

4.1.2   Overview

As it turns out, the above goals are met by automating a number of open source tools which are normally operated by hand by digital investigators. The role of the digital investigator changes in this process, as shown in Fig. 4.2. His task is to prepare digital evidence for the tactical investigator. A tactical investigator is then able to find evidence without further interaction. The digital investigator is on request available for advanced specific analyses.

ocfa has been released as an open source project on sourceforge and is still under development. Current large investigations indicate that it is a useful addition to the current existing forensic tools.

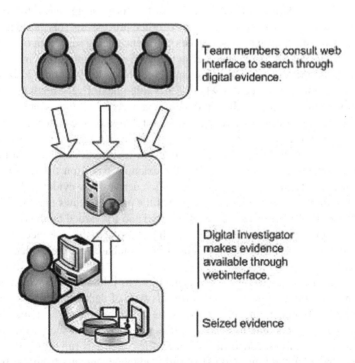

Team members consult web interface to search through digital evidence.

Digital investigator makes evidence available through webinterface.

Seized evidence

Fig. 4.2   Processing digital seized evidence using OCFA

4.2   Technical Description

This chapter describes the approach to the problem of automating digital forensics tasks. One of the goals of these tasks is to extract embedded evidence from digital media and present it to an indexer in a format suitable for processing by that indexer. The second goal is to do feature extraction on the evidence to allow for analysis of metadata. Such an analysis may give interesting results for the investigation. The emphasis is on the embedded data extraction. Once embedded evidence is isolated from the containing evidence, extracting features from it is easy. The next section discusses on a fairly high abstraction level how the unpacking and extraction is handled by OCFA. This is also one of the key aspects of OCFA, the ability to recursively process data as long as embedded evidence is being derived.

4.2.1   Recursive Processing of Data

Much evidence is, intentionally or not, obscured by being embedded in containing files. Figure 4.3 shows an example of how embedded evidence is stored in a tree like structure. To process such evidence as described above, an iterative process is needed. Every time new evidence is derived, it needs to be inspected to determine whether or not the derived evidence needs further processing. Also, the original evidence itself might still be of interest to other processes. This is depicted in Figure 4.4. This illustration shows a piece of evidence being sent from one module to the other. First of all, some piece of evidence E is submitted to a module, the router, which is able to make a decision based on what is known about E. Based on what is known about E, it decides where E has to go next. Every module may add some information, which we call metadata or features, to E. It then sends E back to the router which determines where to send E next, based on the added information. In the illustration, the digest module, which checks hashes against a database, does not recognize the hash. Since E is not recognized the router sends E to a module which determines the file type of E. In this example based on the file type, the router forwards E to the *antiword* module, which derives new evidence E' from E. E' is dealt with just as its parent E, except that the path it follows may be different from that of E. Both evidences are now inspected and forwarded by the router until the router decides that no module exists which may process the evidence further. In that case, the gathered information is stored in a database and the evidence taken out of the processing chain.

The described process above may be generalized as follows; Tools which operate on a given type of data typically transform this type of data from one format F to another format F' generating one or more new files of type F'. If there exists another tool T which is able to deal with files of type F', and such a tool extract features, text or other embedded files from F'-files, then T is run on F'. If no such tool exists, the default action is to extract all readable characters from the file and

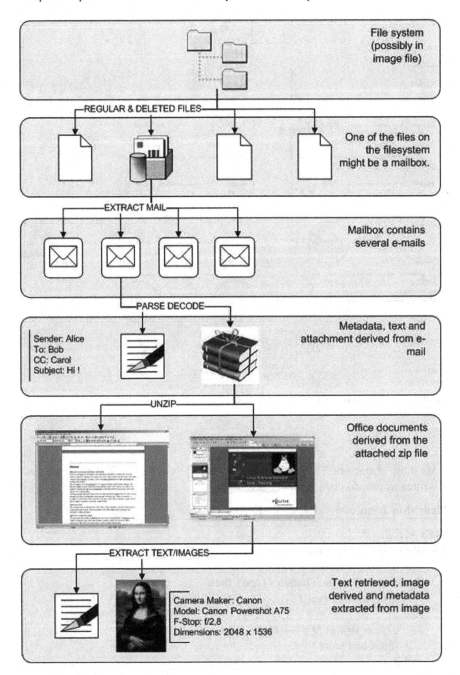

Fig. 4.3 An example of an embedded document

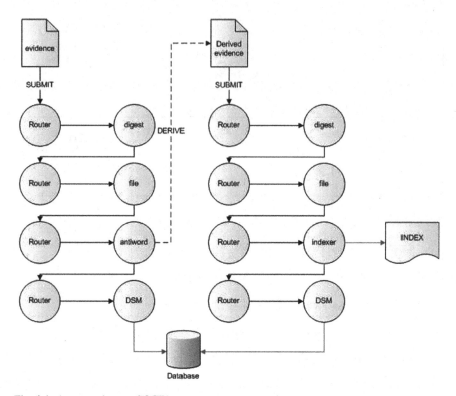

Fig. 4.4 An example run of OCFA

index those characters. The extracted text is stored as a file too. The above process
is written in pseudo code formally below.

Algorithm 1 ProcessEvidence(File F, Tool T)

$T(F) \rightarrow \{F'_0, \ldots, F'_i\}$
for all $f \in \{F'_0, \ldots, F'_i\}$ **do**
    store extracted features of f
    if exist a tool t which handles type f **then**
        ProcessEvidence(f, t)
    else
        extract strings $S(f) \rightarrow f'$
        index and store f'
    end if
end for

OCFA is the framework which goal implements the algorithm described above.
The next chapters discuss the various parts of OCFA in-depth.

4.2.2 The ocfa Library

ocfa is a framework and much of the implementation of the ocfa framework is in the ocfa-library (ocfaLib). The requirement for ocfa to be extendible and to allow modules to communicate makes it necessary to implement some common ground for the modules. In order to achieve this, ocfaLib has been developed. ocfaLib offers the following services to programs using it:

* Messaging between modules such as message objects, serialisation and message endpoints.
* Miscellaneous functionality such as logging and configuration file reading.
* Storage of evidence on the file system and database access.
* Evidence library which contains abstractions to handle the state of evidence and methods to add metadata
* Facade which combines the above mentioned parts in bigger, easier-to-use objects.

4.2.3 The Repository

The repository is a part of the ocfa library which implements the storage interface. The repository offers services such as storing and retrieving of evidence, calculation of hash values and keeping database connections. Every OcfaModule uses the ocfa library and has access to the repository. All derived evidence is stored in the repository, in order to make it available for further processing and analysis by the investigator. The repository is in fact a directory on disk. The top level directory of the repository is called the repository root and is specified in the configuration file.

To avoid problems with funny file- and pathnames all evidence is stored by the SHA1 hash of the data they contain. For example, an empty file would be renamed to da39a3ee5e6b4b0d3255bfef95601890afd80709 in the repository. To avoid cluttering directories with too many files the filename of evidence is split up in three parts. The first two parts which are generated by the splitting of the filename are used in creating a two-level deep directory hierarchy, if it does not exist already. The remainder, or third part, is used as the actual filename within this directory structure. For example, consider the empty file again. The full path to the actual file itself is, relative to the repository root:

/da/39/a3ee5e6b4b0d3255bfef95601890afd80709

Considering the randomness and distribution properties of the SHA1 hash, the directories should be filled evenly with files. Storing a file by its hash ensures that when two or more files have the same contents, those contents are 'shared' by those files. Effectively, every piece of evidence is stored exactly once. Moving files into the repository is done by copying when source evidence is located on another disk or partition. When evidence resides on the same partition, evidence is moved into the repository by setting a hardlink to it, and then unlink the original filename. The latter method is of course superior with respect to speed and storage requirements.

4.2.4 Storage of (Dynamic) Metadata

During the processing of evidence, metadata is updated periodically by modules processing the evidence. This metadata is called dynamic metadata since it is subject to change during the processing of the evidence. The dynamic metadata is stored in XML CLOB's (Character Large Objects) during their processing lifetime. Once the evidence is completely processed and will not change anymore, the XML is parsed and the interesting bits are stored in specific tables in the database to facilitate efficient searches and querying. The relation between the evidence and the metadata describing it is stored in the database. Apart from specific properties of the evidence, the metadata XML also contains important relations like the parent-child relationship between evidence and derived evidence. Another example is the path which is travelled by the evidence through the ocfa processing chain.

4.2.5 Interprocess Communication between Modules

OcfaModules are standalone programs in their own process space. After the framework has been started there are several processes (modules) running. These processes need a way to communicate with each other. After all, they will be sending a lot of work to each other, during the processing of evidence. The implementation of the IPC mechanism uses the Adaptive Communication Environment (ACE) libraries [4]. The only way OcfaModules can communicate with each other is through sending OcfaMessages. OcfaMessages are objects with common properties like sender, receiver and subject for instance.

Basically, there are two main types of messages:

1. Evidence Messages
2. Control messages

Evidence messages provide the means by which modules may send evidence files to each other. Evidence messages contain a handle of the evidence which should be processed by the targeted module. With this handle, the module is able to retrieve the actual file to process from the repository through the store interface. Besides evidence messages there are several control messages which are handled by OcfaModules. Those messages are part of the implementation and won't be discussed here.

4.2.6 The AnycastRelay and the Router

Modules like the AnycastRelay and the Router are considered core modules, since they form the backbone of the architecture. The router decides to which module evidence is sent for processing, while the AnycastRelay delivers the evidence messages to the addressed modules. In order for ocfa to be able to function, at least the

AnycastRelay has to be running, otherwise the OCFA modules don't have a way to sent messages to each other. The router has to be running, otherwise evidences are not routed to modules.

The AnycastRelay gets its name from the terms *broadcast, multicast, unicast* and *anycast*. The following explains the meaning of those terms.

- Broadcast. Messages which are sent with the BROADCAST tag are meant to be sent to *all* instances of *all* module types.
- Multicast. Multicast messages need to be forwarded to *every* module instance of *one designated* module type.
- Anycast. Anycast messages need to be sent to *any one member* of *one designated* module type.
- Unicast. Unicast messages need to be sent to *one designated* module instance.

The network is star-shaped with the AnycastRelay module in the middle, as shown in Fig. 4.5. Many instances of the same module type may connect to the Anycast-relay module, thus spreading the load over many processes/machines. When a module connects to the AnycastRelay module, the first thing it does is sending its module-instance name, wrapped in a message. This message is used by the AnycastRelay module to group modules together which provide the same functionality. Evidence which needs to be processed, normally needs to be processed by a module of a given *type*. It does not matter by which *instance* of the module type the evidence is processed. So, when an evidence message arrives for a given module type, the AnycastRelay may decide to which instance of the module type it should be sent. If an evidence message is

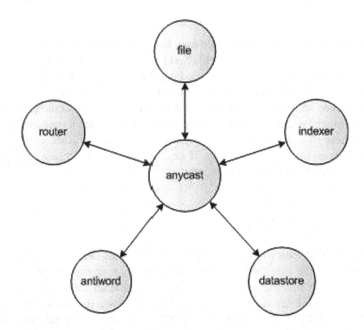

Fig. 4.5 AnycastRelay connected to other modules. Arrows indicate a connection between the modules

destined for a module type for which no module-instance is registered (yet), the messages pending for the module type are stored by the AnycastRelay. This makes it possible to recover from errors when, for example, a module has crashed by restarting it. To the AnycastRelay module it does not matter from which host a module connects. This means that the operating system of the host does not matter either. As long as the connecting module knows how to handle the OcfaMessages it can communicate with other modules. It must be noted however that the AnycastRelay and the OcfaLibrary currently support sending of references to evidence. So a remote host will also need access to the repository to access the actual evidence.

4.2.7 The Router Module

Although it might not be directly obvious, the routing functionality is 'just' an implementation of processEvidence (the method which does the actual processing of an evidence). The evidence itself, however, is never touched. All the information the router needs to make a routing decision is contained within the runtime metadata of the evidence. There is no limit on the different types of metadata to base a routing decision on. Examples include:

- Modified Access Creation (MAC) times
- Mime/File type
- File extension
- Digest source
- Language

Even metadata such as *last module* may be used. This is useful to create fixed chains of evidence processing. Modules add metadata types and their values to evidence. In the case of the digestmodule, for example, the Metatdata type *Digestsource* might be added to the evidence with the value NIST.

The metadata which travels with the evidence contains the path the evidence has travelled through the ocfa modules. The evidence XML contains one or more jobs as its elements. The router adds an empty job to the evidence XML containing its own metadata and debug information, if any. This allows for keeping the parent-child relationship between evidences intact.

4.2.7.1 Rules and the Rulelist

The rulelist is a table on which the router bases its routing decisions, see Table 4.1. The rulelist is stored in a flat file and is loaded by the router at startup. Every line contains a rule. A rule consists of a matching part and an action part. When the metadata of the evidence matches a specific rule, the action is executed for that evidence. The rulelist is modeled after the IP Tables structure. The rulelist contains eight columns, separated by semicolons, which are listed below:

Table 4.1 An example of a rulelist

	Table	Namespace	Type	Value	Last module	FinalAction	Target	Argument
1	default	DNCTR	inodetype	file	DNCTR	ACT_ FORWARD	digest	
2	default	DNCTR	digestsource	UNDEF	DNCTR	ACT_ FORWARD	file	
3	default	DNCTR	mimetype	image/ jpeg	DNCTR	ACT_ FORWARD	exif	
4	default	DNCTR	DNCTR	DNCTR	DNCTR	ACT_ FORWARD	dsm	

- Tablename: Name of a group of rules.
- Namespace: Namespace of the metadata type (next item).
- Type: Name of metadata type.
- Value: Value of metadata type.
- Last module: Name of last processing module.
- FinalAction: Name of step to perform next.
- Target: The module type which should process the evidence next.
- Argument: An optional argument which should be passed along together with the evidence to the next module (target).

The first five columns are used in selecting a rule, whereas the last three columns, FinalAction, Target and Argument, define what to do when a rule matches. The next table shows an example of a small rulelist. The first column contains numbers which are not part of the table itself but are present to refer to.

The meanings of the above rules are, numbered as above:

1. Send any regular file to the digest module.
2. Send any evidence for which the digest module did not find a match (UNDEF) to the filemodule.
3. Send any evidence which has a mimetype 'image/jpeg' to the exif module.
4. Send any evidence which did not match anything up to this rule to the Data Store Module (dsm).

Matches on literal values are exact, except for the Value field, which matches whenever the value matches a substring of the argument to which it is matched against. Support for using regular expressions in the future has been built in. The "don't care" value (DNTCR) matches anything.

4.2.8   Available OCFA Modules

This section gives a short overview of current modules which are available within the OCFA framework. There are three groups of OcfaModules:

- *Extractors.* Extractors are modules which extract metadata from an evidence. For example, the file module determines the mimetype for a given file, and is therefore an extractor.
- *Dissectors.* A dissector is a module which extracts embedded evidence from an (parent) evidence. For example, the unzip module is a dissector, because it dissects zip files and as such extracts the embedded evidence. The new, derived, evidence is submitted by the OCFA library into the processing queue for further analysis by the OCFA framework.
- *Expanders.* An expander is a module which combines metadata from evidence with another source of information. From this action additional metadata may be associated with the evidence. The digest module is an example of an expander since it adds the name of the hashset, if any, in which the hash value occurs.

The next paragraphs describe the most important modules.

4.2.8.1 The Kickstart Module

The module which submits evidence into the OCFA framework is called kickstart. The main argument to kickstart is the path to the evidence. The evidence may be a file or a directory. If the evidence is a file, only that file is submitted to the router.

If the file is directory, the kickstart module recursively submits all files in the directory, including all subdirectories. When submitting the evidence, some additional information has to be provided with it, like a (physical) label number or another identifier to link the evidence file to a real world item (like a hard disk). This information is stored in the database. In normal investigations, evidence which is sent into the framework will consists mainly of hard disk images. However, one might subclass a webspider or usenet reader from the kickstart class to obtain a new module which is able to bootstrap new evidence. In the case of the web spider, one could use the technique to index websites, calculate hashes from content from those sites etcetera. It is easy to see how a similar technique might work with usenet newsgroups. Another possibility, although harder to implement, would be a tcpdump (or other network sniffer) module to perform analysis on a wire tap.

4.2.8.2 Datastore Module

The datastore module (DSM) is the module which is last in the chain of modules and has a direct, thus not through the store library, connection with the OCFA database. The task of the datastore module is to not return the evidence to the router, so effectively taking it out of the OCFA process. The function ality of the datastore module consists of opening a metadata iterator, which is provided by OcfaLib. The iterator is used to visit all embedded metadata and store the values in the designated table in the database. This action makes the metadata more convenient to access for investigators and applications.

4.2.8.3 Miscellaneous Modules

Modules provide the actual functionality which is useful for investigations, like extracting text and unpacking embedded files. Current modules include:

- file: determines the type of an evidencev vbases on libmagic.
- digest: checks the hash of an evidence against a database and adds the result as metadata.
- antiword: retrieves plain text from MicrosoftWord documents.
- pdftotext: retrieves plain text from PDF documents.
- strings: extracts plain text from arbitrary files.
- exif: retrieves EXIF information from JPEG files.
- zip, tar, 7zip: unzip and unpack archive files.
- mailwash: extracts plaintext and attachments from mailboxes and email.
- sleuthkit: extracts evidence (files and unallocated space) from disk images.
- pkr,pgp: extracts metadata information on keyrings.
- tcpflow: extract TCP streams (payload) from PCAP files.
- luceneIndexer: builds an index on evidence.
- win32proxy: sends evidence to a Microsoft Windows machine for processing by native Windows tools. Processed evidence is automatically submitted back into the OCFA processing chain.

Basically, the functionality of modules is implemented in three ways:

1. Modules are simple wrappers around standard Unix/Linux commands using the *popen* system call.
2. Modules use functionality from third party libraries.
3. Modules are developed with build in functionality from the OCFA team.

The filemodule, for example, evolved from a module which spawned the (Unix/Linux) file command to a module which utilized the *libmagic* library. Of course, whenever it's possible, libraries are used, since it is very expensive to spawn a new process for every file that is routed to a module. Secondly, the information, which is returned by a library function, is in most cases immediately usable by the module. This is in contrast with the output of the spawned process, which needs to be parsed, which is error prone and inefficient. For more information on how to develop an OcfaModule, see [6].

4.2.9 Database Layout and Reporting

This section describes the database used by OCFA. The current implementation uses the PostgreSQL DBMS as its back-end. The OCFA database consists of two main groups of tables. One group consists of the 'core' tables which will be discussed first. The other group consists of various tables which are used to store metadata about evidence. The latter group can be added to when new metadata is available, for example, when a new module has been developed. The exact definitions of the tables are beyond the scope of this text, but details can be found in [6].

4.2.9.1 The Core Tables

The core tables store common properties of evidence, such as:

- The casename the evidence belongs to and other administrative information.
- The name of the evidence by which it is stored in the repository.
- The name by which it was originally stored on the suspect device.
- The parent evidence, or derivation path, from which a given evidence was extracted.

4.2.9.2 Additional Metadata Tables

When a new extractor module is deployed there will also be a new metadata type, since this is the point of extractors. Dissectors may add metadata to evidence too. The strings module, for example, adds the extracted character set as metadata to the derived evidence. During a run of ocfa, the metadata is added to the runtime XML of an evidence. Storing it separately in the database is therefore redundant but necessary for efficient analysis. The database structure allows an investigator to combine data from different tables, which makes it possible to ask questions like "give me documents which have been modified in the last week, and for which the mimetype does not match the expected file extension".

Example Generating an Overview of Encountered Mimetypes

To generate an overview of the different types of mimetypes encountered during a run, one only needs to query the metamimetype table. For example an overview such as below generated the data in Table 4.2:

```
select distinct meta, count(*) as nmbr_occurences
from rowmimetype
group by meta
order by nmbr_occurences desc
limit 10
```

The above query can be used on any of the metadata tables. To generate an overview of the encountered file extensions, only the tablename needs to be changed. Substituting *rowmimetype* by *rowfileextension* in the FROM clause of query above gives a similar result for file extensions. as shown in Table 4.3:

Table 4.2 The top 10 of most encountered mime-types, generated by a query on the *rowmimetype* table

meta	nmbr_occurrences
text/x-c++	427
text/plain	316
text/xml	205
text/x-c	78
application/x-perl	59
image/png	56
text/html	32
application/x-zip	30
application/x-empty	25
video/unknown	20

Table 4.3 Output of a similar query ran against the file-extension table

meta	nmbr_occurrences
hpp	269
xml	234
cpp	224
NON	206
png	56
...	...

4.2.9.3   Searching for Specific Values and Creating Export Shell Commands

To see a list of all files which have been labelled by the file module as being pictures the following query is run:

```
select meta, metadataid
from rowmimetype
where meta like 'image/%'
```

The next example shows how such a query might be rewritten to allow an investigator to export files which satisfy certain conditions to an exportdirectory 3[2].

```
select 'cp --parents /var/ocfa/case1/repository'
         || repname || ' /mnt/exportdir/ '
from rowmimetype rmt,
   metadatainfo mdi,
   evidencestoreentity ese
where rmt.metadataid = mdi.metadataid and
   ese.id = mdi.dataid and
   meta like 'image/%';
```

[2] The reader is not expected to readily understand the query and relations involved. The example is included to illustrate a potential application of the database in combination with the repository.

Using pslq, for example, the output of the above query can be piped into a shell which will cause the selected files be copied out of the repository.

4.3   User Interface

The user interface to OCFA consists of two parts. The first is the interface for the digital investigator who has to insert the seized images into OCFA and configure the web interface. The second part is the interface for the tactical investigator, who has to search the unlocked files for evidence.

4.3.1   Command Line Administration Interface

The installation script creates a user ocfa with a few directories in it. The most important, from a user perspective, are:

bin   Directory containing all command line commands and scripts for running OCFA.
cgi-bin Directory containing the cgi-scripts in the web interface.
etc   Directory containing all configuration files.
html   Directory containing all html files. Can be adapted for a customized interface.
inc   Directory containing the header files for those who want to develop or compile new modules for OCFA.
lib   Directory containing all library files necessary to run OCFA.
sbin   Directory containing executables called by those in bin. However, it is possible to run modules individually from this directory

In order to run OCFA, a user first has to create a case. This is done by typing:

ocfa> sudo createcase.pl < *casename* > < *databasepassword* >

This command does a few things:

* It creates a directory structure in the directory /var/ocfa/< *casename* >.

This directory contains the following items:

hashsets   Contains a berkeley database of all digests. This allows OCFA to recognize whether a file was already processed.
index   Directory containing the built index so far.
ppq   Directory used for the persistent storage of messages.
repository Directory containing all items put so far in the digital washing machine.
work   Contains the working directories of all modules.

* It creates a new database named < *casename* >
* It creates a new configuration file < *casename* >.conf in the etc.

• It changes the apache configuration to that a new virtual host *<casename>*.ocfa. loc is added. The apache web server will have to be restarted to take the changed configuration into effect. The new virtual host is automatically configured to check the results for that case. However, the web client has to be made aware that <casename>.ocfa.loc refers to the ip address of the OCFA application server[3].

Now that the case is created the environment OCFACASE should be set to *<casename>*. It is now possible to start OCFA. This is done with the command: `casemon.pl< casename >`.`casemon.pl`, short for casemonitor, is a script that starts the anycast (see section 2.6) and then checks whether any messages exists for non-running modules. If a module receives messages, it is started.

Finally, it is time to put some seize digital evidence into OCFA. This is done by using the command:

kickstart *< casename > < source > < item > < path >*

Source and Item arguments are labels to group the different disk images in OCFA. *< path>*can be a reference to an image file or a directory. It is currently not possible to kickstart a multipart image file directly[4]. It is possible, to kickstart several items after another in OCFA or even simultaneously.

An overview of the OCFA activities can be seen by going to
`http://<casename>.ocfa.loc/cgi-bin/ppqoverview.`
Figure 4.6 shows a screen shot.

The OCFA run is finished when no modules are running anymore. The system can be stopped by giving the `ocfahalt < casename >` command. Some other commands/scripts exist for case administration. The most important ones are `cleanupcase.sh` and `deletecase.sh`

4.3.2   Web Interface

The web interface that is delivered with OCFA is pretty basic. It consists of a browse area and a search area. The browse mode shows all items that have been put in the washing machine. When an item is clicked, the evidence as it was put into OCFA is shown with all the information about it. An example is shown in Figure 4.7.

When output is clicked the information about the directory output, a derivative of test.dd is shown. This way a tactical investigator can browse through the different disk images in a case.

The other option is to search through the data. OCFA uses the lucene indexer [3]. Thus, the lucene syntax can be used. Figure 4.8 shows an example of a search. Both a link to the actual file and a link to the metadata of that file are given for each result. It is possible to use multiple indexes.

---

[3] E.g. by adding a local dns entry of by inserting an entry in the host file of the client/
[4] It is possible, to present a multipart dd or encase image as a dd image using carvfs[2] or convert a multipart encase file to a dd file using ewf[5]

Open Computer Forensics Architecture

Home Index Overview PPQ

PPQ Overview

Module	prio 0	prio 1	prio 2	prio 3	prio 4	prio 5	prio 6	never 7
dsm	0	97	0	0	0	0	0	0
digest	0	0	0	0	0	0	0	0
indexer	0	0	0	0	0	0	0	0
kickstart	0	0	0	0	0	0	0	0
objdump	0	0	0	0	0	0	0	0
zip	0	0	0	0	0	0	0	0
gzip	0	0	0	0	0	0	0	0
router	0	302	0	0	0	0	0	0
file	0	0	0	0	0	0	0	0
tar	0	0	0	0	0	0	0	0

Fig. 4.6 An example view of the running modules in OCFA. Messages queues are shown for each module

4.3.3 Security

The user interface is currently not secure. This means that OCFA must be run in a secure environment. This holds for the network as well as for the physical environment. Another security related issue is how to deal with viruses and other types of malware. Since most part of OCFA is running on Linux, the casual windows viruses will do no damage on the OCFA server itself. It becomes a problem when users download evidence to their machines. Through the user interface this is indeed possible and poses a security issue. In many cases, a tactical investigator is not interested in binary files and office documents can be viewed as plain text in the user interface, so it is tempting to think that the problems are not there. Still, this is an issue which needs to be addressed.

4.4 Discussion

This section reflects our thoughts about the current state of OCFA. The first part evaluates to which extent OCFA meets the desired objectives. Then, future work is considered.

Open Computer Forensics Architecture

Case:	osconf
Source:	aSource
Item:	anItem

HOME INDEX Overview PPQ

Evidence browser

		osconf :: aSource :: anItem :: / test.dd
	output	

Detailed meta information for evidence:

	test.dd	Bekijk
Job	MetaName	MetaValue
kickstart	**stime = 2009-01-26T09:56:00**	**etime = 2009-01-26T09:56:00**
	accesstime	2009-01-26T09:20:43:OcfaModule
	changetime	2008-07-15T13:44:27:OcfaModule
	fsentity-type	reachablenode
	gid	100
	groupreadable	100
	inodetype	file
	modificationtime	2008-07-15T13:44:27:OcfaModule
	size	10001546
	uid	1000
	worldreadable	true
router	**stime = 2009-01-26T09:56:00**	**etime = 2009-01-26T09:56:00**
digest	**stime = 2009-01-26T09:56:05**	**etime = 2009-01-26T09:56:05**
	digestfirst	0
	digestcount	1
	digestsource	UNDEF
router	**stime = 2009-01-26T09:56:05**	**etime = 2009-01-26T09:56:05**
file	**stime = 2009-01-26T09:56:09**	**etime = 2009-01-26T09:56:09**
	mimetop	application
	mimetype	application/octet-stream
	mimeinfo	ocfa_undef
	fileinfo	data
	fileextension	dd
router	**stime = 2009-01-26T09:56:09**	**etime = 2009-01-26T09:56:09**
sleuthkit	**stime = 2009-01-26T09:56:13**	**etime = 2009-01-26T09:56:13**
router	**stime = 2009-01-26T09:56:13**	**etime = 2009-01-26T09:56:13**

Fig. 4.7 An example of how evidence is represented. The name of the file is test.dd. According to the file module, the type is application data and not much is known about it. A directory is derived from it by the sleuthkit module

4.4.1   Evaluation

To what extent did OCFA meet its objective? Practical experience on real cases have shown that OCFA can be used to unlock terabytes of computer images and files and can built an index of text data on them. The following paragraphs focus on the different boundary conditions as described in section 1.1.

Chain of Evidence. Following and reproducing the chain of evidence is extremely simple and works very well. Each piece of evidence carries a trace of all the modules it went through.

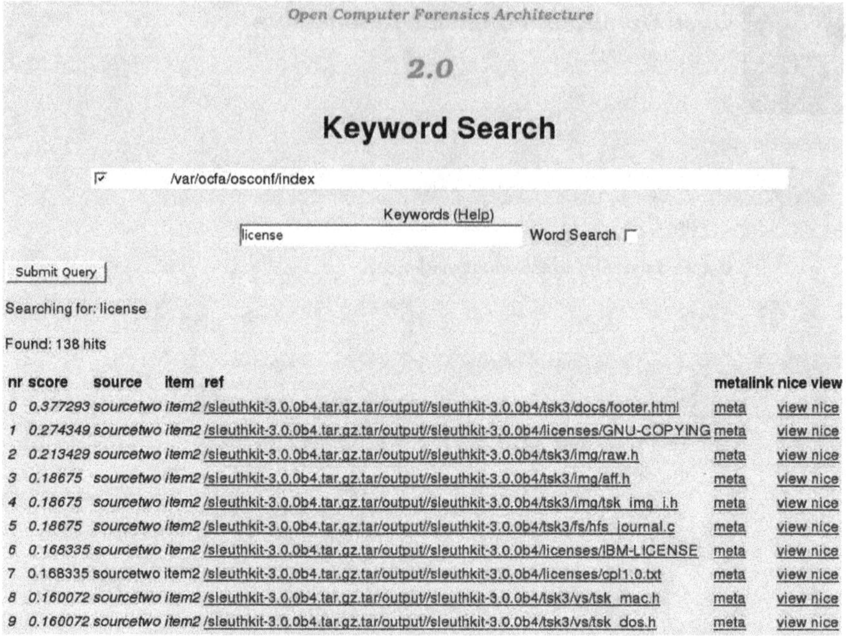

Fig. 4.8 An example of searching in OCFA

Openness. Besides the point that OCFA is open source, the results of OCFA are
stored in a postgres database, a directory tree and a lucene index. The directory
tree and database are already used, for instance, to export images to specialized
image viewers. An external application only needs to have a postgresql database
connection to get to the data.

Scalability. In theory, it should be easy to have OCFA run on multiple platforms for
one single case. However, this has not been tested on a real case. One issue that
should be considered is that, although the modules run as separate processes and
the database can run on a separate machine, the directory tree should be available to all modules. Using a network file server can have a detrimental effect on
performance. Experiments with smb as a file sharing mechanism turned out to
create errors during an OCFA run.

Stability. The OCFA infrastructure is remarkably stable. Modules can crash without
bringing down the whole system as describe in section 2.6. However, no provi-
sions are currently made when a module 'hangs', which means that it keeps on
processing without crashing and without returning anything. Another issue arose
when the sleuthkit module did not process certain images. When the kickstarted
image cannot be processed, the whole chain stops nothing actually happens.

Modularity. Creating new modules and putting them in OCFA is easy. Currently
only a c++ API exists, but a Java version is currently being tested.

Ease of Use. The web interface is easy to use but very primitive. Some work still has to be done on it. Other issues which arose are the different states OCFA can be in when something goes unexpectedly during a run, and the size of the database. These problems are all solvable but currently require intimate knowledge of OCFA. OCFA can be run without looking at the code, but you still need to be familiar with its quirks.

4.4.2   Future Work

One of the biggest issues in the adaptation of OCFA is how hard it is to actually run it while juggling with terabytes of seized data. Currently, work is done to create a graphical user interface to facilitate this problem.

Other work that is being started is the FIVES project [1]. The project will deliver modules that can help in detecting child pornography. Other planned deliverables are user interfaces for viewing pictures and movies. OCFA will be used as forensic engine.

Another issue is the needed level of support. Regardless how well developed OCFA will be, police organizations will need professional support. Unfortunately, providing support on software is not a task for our police organization. Currently we are negotiating with commercial vendors who can provide software license agreements for OCFA.

References

1. Garcia J et al (2008) Forensic image and video examination support (fives). http://fives.kau.se
2. Team Digital Expertise. (2008) Libcarvpath. http://ocfa.sourceforge.net/libcarvpath/
3. The Apache Software Foundation. (2009) Lucene. http://lucene.apache.org/
4. Huston SD, Johnson JCE, Syyid U (2003) The ACE Programmer's Guide: Practical Design Patterns for Network and Systems Programming. Addison-Wesley/Pearson Education
5. Kloet B, Metz J, Mora R-J, Loveall D, Schreiber D (2008) Libewf. https://www.uitwisselplatform.nl/projects/libewf/
6. Vermaas O (2008) The open computer forensic architecture. Master's thesis, University College Dublin, Forensic Computing and Cybercrime Investigations

Chapter 5
Open Source Live Distributions for Computer Forensics

Giancarlo Giustini, Mauro Andreolini, and Michele Colajanni

Abstract Current distributions of open source forensic software provide digital investigators with a large set of heterogeneous tools. Their use is not always focused on the target and requires high technical expertise. We present a new GNU/Linux live distribution, named CAINE (*Computer Aided INvestigative Environment*) that contains a collection of tools wrapped up into a user friendly environment. The CAINE forensic framework introduces novel important features, aimed at filling the interoperability gap across different forensic tools. Moreover, it provides a homogeneous graphical interface that drives digital investigators during the acquisition and analysis of electronic evidence, and it offers a semi-automatic mechanism for the creation of the final report.

5.1 Introduction

Computer Forensics is the science for the identification, extraction, collection, analysis, documentation and protection of digital evidence. The discipline extends the investigative techniques to any digital device in order to determine the potential evidence having legal value [18]. Digital evidence started being taken into account in court in the late seventies. In the early days, the judges considered such evidence not very different from traditional evidence. However, the continuous progress of the digital technology pointed out the difficulty of a widely accepted classification [4]. In this paper, we consider the definition of digital evidence given by the Scientific Working Group on Digital Evidence as "any information with evidentiary value that is either stored or transmitted in a digital format" [14].

G. Giustini (✉), M. Andreolini, and M. Colajanni
Department of Information Engineering, University of Modena and Reggio Emilia, Italy
e-mails: giancarlo.giustini@unimore.it; mauro.andreolini@unimore.it;
michele.colajanni@unimore.it

E. Huebner and S. Zanero (eds.), *Open Source Software for Digital Forensics*, 69
DOI 10.1007/978-1-4419-5803-7_5, © Springer Science+Business Media, LLC 2010

Most legal structures and specific competencies on digital evidence arose in the early eighties, when the laboratories of FBI and other US agencies developed software programs to examine evidence on computers. In particular, to respond adequately to the growing demand of investigators and public prosecutors, the FBI established the CART (Computer Analysis and Response Team), with the specific task of conducting tests on computers [17]. Although CART is unique inside the FBI, its functions and its overall organization are now replicated in many other private agencies in the United States and other nations. One of the most significant events in the Computer Forensic discipline is the publication by the Department of Justice of the United States of a set of guidelines (updated in 2004) that became a de facto standard for their accuracy, completeness and authority [2].

The response of law enforcement agencies to digital evidence requires investigators and officers to follow proper forensic procedures that include four main phases: *collection, examination, analysis, and reporting* [1]. Nowadays, each phase can be carried out through the assistance of some specific forensic software, where the main distinction is between proprietary packages and open source tools. The focus of this paper is on the latter area. We should observe that open source and free tools are seldom designed to interoperate with other programs and they do not share data and results with the software in charge of the successive phase. Moreover, the compilation of a written report that outlines the overall examination process and the most pertinent recovered information remains another big issue for digital investigators [11, 12]. This report is typically obtained through a complex and manual process where the digital investigator has to save and mix together heterogeneous software output, documentation and personal comments in one or more text files. As a further consequence of the lack of software interoperability, the report compilation process cannot be automated, and remains an open issue.

We present a novel live distribution named CAINE (*Computer Aided INvestigative Environment*) that aims to overcome some of the most critical limits of forensic distributions. It offers a complete forensic environment that is organized to integrate existing software tools as software modules and to provide a friendly graphical interface. We do not aim to propose "yet another forensic tool" or a framework for collecting open source programs because many forensic distributions already exist (e.g., Helix [16], FCCU [25], DEFT [23]). The main design objectives that CAINE aims to guarantee are the following:

- an interoperable environment that supports the digital investigator during the four phases of the digital investigation;
- a user friendly graphical interface;
- a semi-automated compilation of the final report.

The remaining part of this chapter is organized as following. In Section 2, we discuss related work and we evidence the main advancements of CAINE with respect to other open source distributions. In Section 3, we present the main four phases of digital investigation according to the Department of Justice guidelines [2]. In Section 4, we describe the architecture of the CAINE distribution with a special focus on the software wrapper and the interface. In Section 5, we describe the popular forensic tools included in the present version of CAINE. In Section 6, we describe the reporting phase that in CAINE can be carried-out in a semi-automatic way. In Section 7, we outline the evolution of the CAINE version and the main testing activities that were carried out to achieve the current version. In Section 8, we conclude with some final remarks.

5.2   Related Work

The main requirement of any digital forensic investigation is to preserve the integrity of the digital device under examination. This means that the content of the main memory and of any peripheral storage device must not be altered by the presence of the forensic tool. While all current existing forensic live distributions ([16], [25], [23]) guarantee integrity (with the notable exception of the swap issue which will be discussed in Section 7.3), there has been little effort to provide the user with a friendly environment that conforms to the general guidelines suggested by the American Department of Justice [2].

The large majority of open source distributions are more concerned with system oriented issues, such as providing reasonably up-to-date software packaging, tracking down the required dependencies, but paying less attention to the integration issues. The typical result is an environment that requires competencies in multiple fields (operating system kernels, drivers, file systems, security, forensic). Even worse, there are few if any efforts to integrate different tools and data exchanges. (Just to give an example, there is no common evidence of a representation format.) Hence, highly specialized human effort or multiple interventions are necessary to carry out the whole process of forensic investigation. Although we are in favor of this traditional approach, we have also to observe that the spread of digital devices cannot be counterbalanced by a parallel and instantaneous diffusion of high level competencies in any case of digital investigation. The CAINE project aims to facilitate the use of open source tools to a wider community, still preserving the total satisfaction of Computer Forensic investigation requirements.

We decided to implement the CAINE distribution through the use of open source software. There are several reasons behind this choice. The open source universe owns a large slice of the Computer Forensics software market. Although the open source tools do not provide a commercial certification of their capabilities, the presence of a global community ensures a continuous software development, feedback and improvement. This ensures that the software bundled with the distribution will be always reasonably up-to-date. Furthermore, thanks to a constant team work and code sharing, the most important and used forensic open source software guarantees transparency and repeatability of the investigation process. By publishing source code, the Computer Forensic community can examine and validate the procedures used to produce digital evidence. This model allows a very low error rate because all bug fixes would be made public, and a stable code base can be developed fairly quickly.

Unfortunately, the open source model presents even some drawbacks. Decentralized collaboration works best when the software users are also experienced programmers that can sustain and share the development and maintenance efforts.

The typical users do not necessarily have the required background to collaborate directly with upstream development. Another problem is the scarce integration between open source forensic applications written by different, non-cooperating and sometimes competitive communities. This poor integration causes the execution of different standalone processes during the digital investigation, and forces the investigators to manually gather results from heterogeneous sources (e.g., Helix [16]). Furthermore, the large majority of these applications (e.g., *TheSleuthKit* framework [21], Foremost [28], Scalpel [29] to cite the most famous) offers a command line interface, which is non intuitive and error prone for users with just Windows-like interface experience. For these reasons, several investigators are served by proprietary software manufacturers (e.g., *EnCase* [26]) that guarantee usability through a user friendly environment. The problems of carrying out Computer Forensics through closed source software are well known by the specialized community[1] [19] [20].

The main role of CAINE is to reduce the gap between existent upstream developers and users without in-depth technological knowledge. This objective is pursued through two directions: (a) by interacting with upstream development with the goal of creating a clean, correct, as bug-free as possible distribution; (b) by improving the scarce interoperability across different pieces of software developed by different communities.

The CAINE project aims to provide a not invasive, user friendly, semi-automatic environment for forensic activities with the following main features:

- software modularity that guarantees an easy extension of its core functions;
- usability with the aim of capturing a large, possibly un-technical, user base;
- scalable acquisition process;
- integration of heterogeneous software components into a unique suite;
- final report facilities which are customizable with existing templates.

5.3 Phases of Digital Investigation

The CAINE environment guides the digital investigator to follow the four main phases of a Computer Forensics investigation: information gathering, collection, analysis, and reporting. The first three phases and the CAINE interface are described here, while the reporting phase is presented in Section 6.

5.3.1 Information Gathering

Information gathering from computer data storage devices plays a key role in Computer Forensics. Before collecting the evidence and creating the forensic image

---

[1]"If security is to be taken seriously, only those operating systems should be used, whose source code has been published and checked, since only then can it be determined with certainty what happens to the data." *Temporary Committee on the ECHELON Interception System.* European Parliament, 4 May 2001.

from the devices, investigators must obtain precise information on device geometry, hidden partition metadata, unknown file systems and ambient data sectors. The CAINE interface is built to offer a small and functional graphical interface to gain all information needed from the connected devices, mainly through several command-line tools from TheSleuthKit and some useful BASH scripts.

5.3.2   Collection

The collection of electronic evidence represents the most critical phase of digital investigation [6]. Electronic evidence is, by its nature, fragile because it may be altered, damaged, or destroyed by improper handling or examination. For this reason, special precautions should be taken by the investigator to document, collect, preserve, and examine the electronic evidence. Any failure in this phase causes serious consequences to the extent that the entire forensic analysis may become useless or lead the investigation to an inaccurate conclusion [1, 2]. Hence, it is mandatory that digital investigators use specific programs to perform a fail-safe acquisition of the electronic evidence.

CAINE supports a large variety of file systems and adopts the most severe policies for device mounting. To this purpose, the CAINE distribution mounts all the connected device in read-only mode, it does not allow direct execution of any binaries on the mounted file systems (using the *noexec* option), and it does not update i-node access times on this file system (*noatime* option). These options are set for all the file systems supported by CAINE: FAT(8/16/32), NTFS, Ext2/Ext3, Hfs/Hfs+ and Reiserfs.

5.3.3   Examination and Analysis

The collection phase is followed by two sub-phases (examination and analysis) where CAINE assists the digital investigator in making visible the overall content of the electronic evidence visible and in explaining its origin and significance.

The *examination* phase should document the content and the state of the whole electronic evidence. It has the purpose of discovering what is contained in the evidence, included the search for information that may be hidden or obscured. Once the entire information is recovered and visible, the digital investigator can begin the process of data reduction [6, 14].

The *analysis* phase includes the interpretation of the information that has been collected and validated. This is a critical phase because it looks for significance and probative value of the information with respect to the specific case of investigation. It is worth to observe that analysis and examination typically use the same forensic tools, but there is a huge difference in the approach and goals of these two investigation phases. While examination is a technical review and a summary of the collected files performed by the digital investigator, the analysis aims to exploit digital evidences for forensic purposes [6].

5.4   CAINE Architecture

CAINE is a complete forensic environment that is organized as an integration of existing and novel software modules. It includes the most important forensic programs that have been selected from the open source Computer Forensics community. The programs are installed into the system and connected with the CAINE wrapper that guarantees modularity and extensibility, and provides the user with a graphical interface and assistance for data collection, examination, analysis and final report generation (Fig. 5.1).

5.4.1   Software Wrapper

The forensic software modules are installed inside the main interface that wraps all of them. This choice guarantees a real software integration and a continuous control of every investigation phase. Each program inside CAINE is executed through a set of customized BASH commands embedded into Perl code. The main interface is designed as a GTK2-Perl project: a main file represents the first menu screen; the methods and procedures are included inside several packages that are invoked from the menu.

The CAINE wrapper is written in Perl v. 5.10 and manages the forensic process from the collection of digital evidence to the semi-automatic report compilation. The choice of Perl is motivated by its portability, flexibility and widespread use [3]. Moreover, Perl scripts are used extensively within the computer security

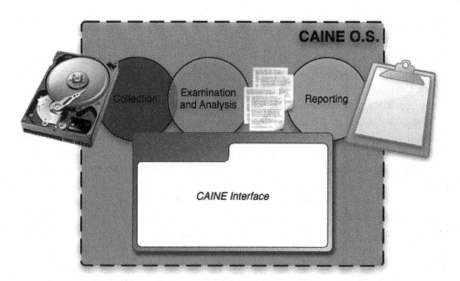

Fig. 5.1 Investigation phases in CAINE

community (e.g. TheSleuthKit and AIR). The Perl part is a sort of "nutshell" of the program execution, where several fork functions control program execution and conclusion, and maintain parallelisms between different software modules. The core of the invocation process is represented by BASH scripts that execute the programs and allow a high level integration by managing software input, output, records and errors. This layered structure guarantees flexibility and modularity to CAINE. For example, the integration of a new forensic software inside CAINE requires just few lines of Perl code, and the correspondent BASH command to execute the selected program.

The choice of creating a wrapper to integrate different software and tools is related to the main purpose of CAINE that is to guarantee full functionality of the available tools and their usability through a user friendly graphical interface and a semi-automated report building tool.

The CAINE wrapper is embedded into a customized Linux-based operating system that is built from the standard desktop version of Ubuntu Linux 8.04. The motivation of starting from Ubuntu Linux is to guarantee the integrity of the system and a frequent update check of the installed packages, thanks to Canonical's philosophy for facilitating the continued growth and development of the free software community. CAINE merges the wrapper inside an Ubuntu partition. The operating system was modified from a minimal Ubuntu installation for a twofold use: it can be booted into a PC under investigation as a live CD; it can be installed into a forensic laboratory PC as a permanent operating system. The CAINE distribution offers all the main commodities of Ubuntu: easy-to-use environment, highly customizable architecture, reliable interfaces and an enhanced package-oriented software distribution system. The GNOME desktop offers a well known and efficient GUI to the digital investigator.

The installation process is fully configurable and automated through a series of shell scripts. After the installation of all accessory modules, the live CD distribution is created through a reliable backup program that automatically builds up a live distribution from the installed Ubuntu version and stored files.

5.4.2 Graphical Interface

The desktop environment is based on GNOME. CAINE uses a Perl interface to the GTK2 graphics library **GTK2-Perl** to meet GNOME's graphical requirements [9, 10]. GTK2-Perl is a set of Perl bindings for Gtk+ 2.x, created to write GNOME applications through a manageable object-oriented syntax.

By following the typical guidelines [1] of a forensic case management, we divide the main interface in four parts (Figure 5.2): information gathering (Grissom Analyzer), collection, examination/analysis, and report (final documentation). We create a usable environment to guide investigators during the digital investigation. An investigator must select the report creation button to create a temporary file and set the initial time stamp of the case. This information will be reported in the documentation.

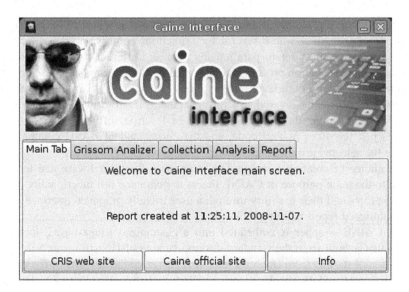

Fig. 5.2 CAINE interface

After the creation of the report file, it is possible to use the forensic tools. The interface pattern has been demonstrated to be intuitive through checks with technical experts and forensic not-technical experts. The five tabs are disposed so to guide the main forensic steps of a digital investigation.

All CAINE software modules are executed through buttons and menus. As we think that graphical interfaces are important to extend digital investigation, we implement front-end for all the forensic tools embedded in CAINE, including Foremost and Stegdetect that are distributed with a command line interface.

5.5   Tools Integrated in CAINE

The current version of the CAINE distribution includes various popular tools that can be used in one or more phases of the digital investigation. (We remark that additional tools can be easily integrated into CAINE thanks to its modular architecture design.)

5.5.1   Information Gathering

- **Grissom Analyzer**. This is a collection of three important commands for information gathering of TheSleuthKit that are included in CAINE: **mmls,** a command that displays the layout of the partitions in a volume system, including partition tables and disk labels; **img_stat** displays the information of an image file; **fsstat** displays the details associated with a file system, including the details from the Super Block, such as mount times and related features. The CAINE interface captures the output of all these commands, displays the logs in a separate window and saves all the information in a temporary file that will be used by the reporting tool.

- **LRRP**. *LRRP.sh* is a BASH script that gathers information on the devices. It can operate in two modes. If the investigation is based on a live CD, this script extracts useful information about the hardware configuration of the suspected machine, as well as specific information on the device that the investigator intends to acquire. If the investigation is carried out through a forensic workstation, this script identifies the machine of the operator and the operating system, and it extracts all information about the analysed device.

5.5.2 Collection

- **AIR**. Automated Image & Restore (AIR) is an open source application that provides a front-end to dd/dcfldd. It supports MD5/SHAx hashes, SCSI tape drives, imaging over a TCP/IP network, splitting images, and detailed session logging. The CAINE interface implements a modified version of AIR to guarantee software integration and usability.
- **Guymager**. Guymager is a forensic imaging tool that handles standard raw (dd) files and Encase files. It uses a high speed multi-threaded engine and it has a user friendly graphical interface.
- **Terminal with log save**. During the forensic image collection, the investigator can use the CAINE graphical interface, but he can also perform a manual collection through the dd command activated in a terminal window. In this instance, CAINE offers the possibility to use a terminal window with automatic output saving that is stored inside a temporary file, managed by the CAINE reporting tool.

5.5.3 Examination and Analysis

- **Foremost and Scalpel**. CAINE provides the investigator with Foremost and Scalpel that are data carving programs recovering files based on their headers, footers, and internal data structures. Scalpel is a modified and better version of Foremost 0.69, and works directly on a drive or on image files, such as those generated by dd, Safeback, Encase. Both programs are provided with a tailored interface that allows multiple windows for input/output selection and direct access to the user/help manual [28] [29].

- **Autopsy**. The Autopsy Forensic Browser is a graphical interface for TheSleuthKit tools that are originally based on command lines. They allow a digital investigator to analyze Windows and UNIX disks, and related file systems such as NTFS, FAT, UFS1/2, Ext2/3. CAINE maintains the same browser-like interface of Autopsy, but it controls output production and report generation through BASH scripts.
- **SFDumper**. It is a Bash script which can retrieve all the files of a chosen type (e.g. .doc or .jpg), regardless if they are active, deleted or unallocated. It automatically runs Foremost for carving, and Sleuthkit for deleted files retrieval. It then eliminates duplicated files by comparing the SHA256 hashes of the carved files and the active and deleted files. Thanks to carving, files renamed with a different extension can be easily identified. Moreover, it is possible to expand the Foremost configuration file inside the script to add new extensions, and to carry out a keyword search on the extracted files. The script can work on an image file or can be directly applied to a device.
- **Stegdetect**. It is an open source tool for steganography that is useful to discover hidden information in stored images. CAINE adds a graphical interface to the command in the main interface, and it provides also an alternative graphical front-end *Xsteg*. Stegdetect works through a simple syntax that asks the user to provide a directory in which JPEG images are stored. The graphical interface allows the investigator to select a folder in which suspected steganographic pictures are stored. At the end of the process, the interface saves the results in a temporary file, that is ready to be included in the final investigation report.
- **Ophcrack**. This is a famous program for password exploiting. CAINE does not provide *rainbow tables* to Ophcrack because of memory space problems of the live CD version, however it guarantees full compatibility between Ophcrack and the CAINE distribution. This program comes with a graphical interface that is integrated within CAINE.

5.6 Report Building Phase

The possibility of a simple communication of the results of the digital analysis is an important feature provided by CAINE at the end of the investigation. The idea is to create a well structured and understandable report, and to avoid unnecessary technical details and digressions. During the phases of collection, examination and analysis, a digital investigator can write notes and reports that record the main characteristics of the examination process, some partial conclusions and the most important recovered information. These examination notes must be preserved until the end of the investigation case, when they are set up in a clear and complete report. We recall that a digital investigator may be required to testify about not only the examination results, but also about the validity of the procedure conduct and his qualifications to carry out the investigation.

Existing open source forensic programs are affected by two main problems: they typically produce only a small synthesis of the executed procedures; they tend to

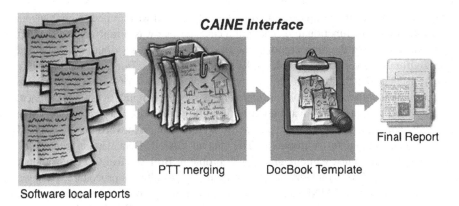

Software local reports

Fig. 5.3 Incremental building of the final report

generate a large number of text files that must be handled manually by the digital investigator (e.g., Autopsy). To address these issues, CAINE introduces a semiautomatic method for combining the output of different and heterogeneous software tools and assisting a digital investigator in the process of assembling the final documentation possibly by following the template(s) required by some law enforcement agencies. All the CAINE features are highly customizable hence it is possible to solve the problems related to the manual compilation of the final documentation by considering different Country laws.

In CAINE, we use the **Perl Template Toolkit** [8] to manage the final reporting process. PTT is a fast, flexible and extensible template processing system that can help a digital investigator to record and aggregate every notable contribution in temporary files and pipeline outputs in a final report. The reporting process is outlined in Figure 5.3. As every tool produces a written output and a sort of minimal report, we make extensive use of the PTT facilities to produce a report from an initial template. At the end of the investigation, all temporary backups are "pipelined" into one text file through **DocBook** [7] SGML, that is a highly customizable markup language for technical documentation. At the end of the investigation process, the CAINE user can produce a final documentation simply by pressing a button from the main inter face. The invoked function converts the SGML DocBook file in one of the following formats: RTF or HTML.

5.7   CAINE Evolution and Validation

5.7.1   Beta Release

The first Beta version of CAINE was distributed for testing to five components of the research lab, of which just two of them were computer forensics experts.

This version was not completely forensic compliant, and was limited to guarantee a minimum level of functionality. The graphical interface was primitive, and CAINE did not provide all the present tools. The first CAINE-Beta distribution was booted on a virtualized version of Windows XP running on a MacBook through Vmware Fusion. This distribution worked correctly, but it lacked of some basic media management software that was considered necessary to a digital investigator. Hence, we decided to rebuild the distribution by installing some open source audio, video and text software, such as Totem, Audacity, Epdfview and Abiword that guaranteed an adequate operative environment. The second CAINE-Beta version passed the first virtualization test without any notable problem. Both the live CD environment and the hard disk version worked well including the installation procedure. Then we decided to burn the CAINE distribution image and to test it on different machines, including an Acer dual-boot laptop (model 9300), a Sony Windows-Vista laptop (model VGNFZ21M), and on an Olidata Desktop Windows XP PC (Athlon64, model 3000+), without noticeable difference from the first series of tests: both live CD and installation worked flawlessly. After several tests on several real and virtualized architectures, we finally produced the first stable version.

5.7.2   Early Releases

As CAINE passed the functionality tests, we carried out a "field test" experiment through the CAINE 0.1 version. The goal was to estimate the effectiveness of the CAINE features in two emulated computer forensic investigations from the literature.

The first case is presented as a typical "search and find" analysis of a collected floppy disk image, in which investigators must recover some relevant evidence related to a specific fictional case [22]. The second case is a file recovery scenario, in which we analyzed a 512 MB pen drive, FAT32 formatted, containing some deleted JPEG images and many other irrelevant media files. We examined a huge set of images and we recovered the deleted files. At the end of the process, CAINE produced documentation with only the necessary information according to the investigation guidelines. We resolved the cases by means of the Helix-based tools that is, AIR, Autopsy and Foremost. At the end of the forensic process, CAINE produced a complete and clear documentation of the case management that avoids manual report compilation. On the other hand, in the "Helix scenario", which is typical of open source forensic frameworks, a digital investigator is forced to save the output of every used software, to integrate it and to produce the final report manually. The response about the qualitative analysis of CAINE from the two external computer forensic experts was quite positive.

We released the first downloadable version of CAINE for the public on October 2008, and then we continued to work on improving existing standards and management of the investigative report. Thanks to the joint efforts of developers, testers and the open-source community, version 0.1 passed to 0.2 and later to 0.3. The second release corrected some bugs regarding compatibility with SFDumper and the CAINE interface, while the 0.3 stable version provided compatibility with AFF and EWF formats. AFF is an extensible open format for the storage of disk images and related forensic metadata designed by Brian Carrier, and EWF is used by EnCase commercial suite, produced of Guidance Software. We also improved the usability of CAINE by installing the latest version stable of Autopsy and TSK, properly interfaced with the latest forensic formats.

5.7.3   Swap Issue and Current Release

At a certain point, we realized that the version 0.3 of CAINE suffered from a common problem of many forensic distributions based on Linux, especially Ubuntubased: it writes on a swap partition already present on the booted system. This problem is due to an automatic procedure inherited from the Ubuntu service initialization system, and affects a Linux system in which a partition is allocated as swap space. In this case the swap space is automatically recognized and activated during the phase of boot by the *swapon* command. When this bug was reported, it was discovered that other forensic distributions, such as DEFT version 4.0, Plainsight 0.1 and For-Lex 1.2.0, were affected by the same problem. The problem was solved in version 0.4, implementing a strategy that prevents the system to activate the swap. We also changed the partition table in /etc/fstab by setting the value *noauto* in the mount options field, thus preventing any forced activation from the system.

Besides fixing the swap problem, CAINE-v0.4 adds a multi-language report saving, thus offering the possibility to implement different languages in the report template.

5.8   Conclusions

CAINE is a novel forensic environment that offers important features to suppor digital investigators. CAINE contains the same familiar tools maintained by the open source forensic community. Moreover, it offers several graphical interfaces to command-line programs that create a user friendly environment through which a digital investigator can easily control the whole collection and analysis process. The forensic software integration provided by CAINE leads a digital investigator to a more structured case management. The graphical interface assists a digital investigator during the collection, examination and analysis phases until the final report generation that offers automatic report integration based on the output of different tools. This last step is not supported by any current forensic distribution, and represents one of the most appreciated CAINE functionality. Special attention has been posed to the extensibility of CAINE tools and reporting functions because every country has its investigation needs and rules. As an alternative to commercial closed source programs (e.g., EnCase [26], FTK [27]), CAINE is a flexible and extendible distribution. It manages every installed software as a module, so that a new tool can be easily integrated into CAINE through few lines of Perl code. This architecture guarantees several possible evolutions of CAINE that may take into account different national legislations and best practices.

References

1. US Department of Justice (2001) Electronic Crime Scene Investigation: A Guide for First Responders. US Department of Justice
2. US Department of Justice (2004) Forensic Examination of Digital Evidence: A Guide for Law Enforcement. US Department of Justice
3. Carvey H (2207) Perl Scripting for Windows Security: Live Response, Forensic Analysis, and Monitoring. Syngress Publishing Inc.
4. Lacouture PV (1996) Discovery and the use of computer-based information in litigation. Rhode Island Bar Journal
5. Carrier B (2005) File System Forensic Analysis. Addison Wesley Professional
6. Solomon MG, Barrett D, Broom N (2005) Computer Forensics JumpStart. Sybex
7. Walsh N, Muellner L. (2007) DocBook 5.0: The Definitive Guide. O'Reilly
8. Chamberlain D, Cross D, Wardley A (2003) Perl Template Toolkit. O'Reilly
9. Foy BD, Phoenix T, Schwartz RL (2005) Learning Perl, 4th Edition. O'Reilly
10. Nagler R (2004) Extreme Programming in Perl. Robert Nagler
11. International Association of Chiefs of Police Advisory Committee for Police Investigative Operations (2005) Best Practices for Seizing Electronic Evidence. PricewaterhouseCoopers LLP
12. Nolan R, O'Sullivan C, Branson J, Waits C (2005) First Responders Guide to Computer Forensics. CERT Training and Education
13. The Internet Crime Complaint Center (2007) 2006 Internet Fraud Crime Report. National White Collar Crime Center & FBI
14. Computer Crime and Intellectual Property Section - Criminal Division (2002) Searching and Seizing Computers and Obtaining Electronic Evidence in Criminal Investigations. US Department of Justice
15. Geiger M, Cranor LF (2005) Counter-Forensic Privacy Tools - A Forensic Evaluation. Carnegie Mellon University
16. Gleason BJ, Fahey D (2006) Helix 1.7 for Beginners. http://www.e-fense.com/
17. FBI: Computer Analysis and Response Team (2007) http://www.fbi.gov/hq/lab/org/cart.htm.
18. Robbins J (2007) An Explanation of Computer Forensics. http://www.computerforensics.net/forensics.htm.
19. Richard Ford R (2007) Open vs. Closed: Which Source is More Secure? ACM Queue, February 2007
20. Hiong GS (2004) Open source vs commercial apps: the differences that matter. ZDNet Asia, October 2004
21. The Sleuth Kit. http://www.sleuthkit.org/.
22. Honeynet. http://www.honeynet.org/scans/scan24/.
23. DEFT v3. http://deft.yourside.it/
24. Helix Live CD. http://www.e-fense.com/helix/
25. FCCU GNU/Linux Forensic Boot CD. http://www.lnx4n6.be/
26. EnCase Forensic. http://www.guidancesoftware.com/
27. Forensic Toolkit. http://www.accessdata.com/Products/ftk2test.aspx.
28. Foremost. http://foremost.sourceforge.net/
29. Scalpel: A Frugal, High Performance File Carver. http://www.digitalforensicssolutions.com/Scalpel/

Chapter 6
VALI: A Visual Correlation Tool Based on Vector Clocks

Roberto Gomez, Julio Cesar Rojas, and Erika Mata

Abstract The systems that are able to detect suspicious or malicious activities are a fundamental component in the security process of every organization. These systems generate alerts that correspond to individual events and, in general, these systems do not show the relationships between them. It is important to examine the security data within their overall context in order to better understand what is happening in our systems. In this work, we present a correlation model based on the concept of vector clocks. We also present a tool that is our implementation of this correlation mechanism. This tool can be used by security analysts to generate graphs showing the relationships between the reported events and possibly discovering unknown attack patterns.

6.1 Introduction

Nowadays, we exchange information through a great number of computer networks. These networks play an important role in the way we do business, transactions or personal communication. This communication scheme brings us a lot of benefits but there could be situations that compromise the information's confidentiality, integrity or availability.

Security is the process of maintaining an acceptable level of risk. This process is comprised of the following four parts: evaluation, which is the definition of policies, regulations, budget and technical evaluation of security mechanisms; protection, which is responsible for the application of measures in order to reduce the likelihood of a successful attack; detection, which is the process of intrusion detection to find possible violations to a given security policy; and response, which is the process of

R. Gomez (✉), J.C. Rojas, and E. Mata
Computer Science Department, Instituto Tecnológico y de Estudios Superiores de Monterrey, Campus Estado de México. Carretera a Lago de Guadalupe km. 3.5, Atizapán de Zaragoza, Estado de México, C.P. 51296, México
e-mails: rogomez@itesm.mx; jcrm@itesm.mx; emata@itesm.mx

E. Huebner and S. Zanero (eds.), *Open Source Software for Digital Forensics*, DOI 10.1007/978-1-4419-5803-7_6, © Springer Science+Business Media, LLC 2010

validating the results of the detection process and to make appropriate actions in order to mitigate the impact of the reported intrusions [1].

An intrusion detection system (IDS) is a useful technology capable of detecting suspicious or malicious activities. An *IDS* helps the user to detect some attacks against a particular network. The information generated by an *IDS* has to be revised and analyzed by human beings. If an *IDS* is installed but its alerts are never revised then the system does not bring any benefit [2]. Traditional *IDS* focuses on individual attacks and produces independent alerts in text format. This is done without taking into account that there could possibly be connections between them [15]. Also, it is widely known that these systems could generate a great number of alerts [25].

The great number of alerts and the lack of a mechanism to identify possible relationships between them make it difficult to analyze the reported data. It is possible to detect uncover attacks by relating the generated alerts.

Alert correlation is a complex process which responsibility is to analyze alerts and provide a global view of a network state [26].

This technique is very useful and allows the user to manage great volumes of information. Most of the research done in this area is focused on extracting attack strategies from raw alerts [27].

It is important to determine which events happened before another one so that they could have prepared the necessary conditions in order for the later to be successful.

Information security analysts use attack graphs to do detection, defense and forensic tasks; at the same time, they develop new techniques and tools to get more evidence from computers and networks. Security analysts are continually searching for effective ways to process and visualize network logs so that suspicious activities or hidden attacks can be discovered [9].

Visualization is a technique that shows the relationships between represented elements. Therefore, visualization helps to increase the understanding of security information. It is necessary to present security information in such way that human users can better understand it. Visualization has been applied in many network analysis activities [12].

Vector clocks are a concept used in many distributed applications that range from debugging of distributed systems to group-based text editors. Vector clocks are used to find causality relationships between different events [18, 19].

We apply the concept of vector clocks to correlate security alerts in order to generate graphs. These graphs can show the sequences of events that form a complex attack. This work is organized as follows: in section 2 we explain the concept of alert correlation and its importance in the analysis of security information; in section 3 we present some of the previous works done in the correlation research field; section 4 explains the concept of vector clocks; our correlation model is presented in section 5; in section 6 we present *VALI*, a tool that we developed and that is an implementation of our proposed correlation model; in section 7 we present some of the experiments done with this tool and the obtained results; in section 8 we present a distributed alert correlation model based on the concept of vector clocks that allows us to sort the alerts produced at different sources; and finally, in section 9 we present our conclusions and future work.

6.2   Alert Correlation

The ability to apprehend sophisticated attackers highly depends on the ability of security administrators to follow their traces [2]. With the growing number of computer networks and the huge volumes of data transmitted between them, it has become more complicated to supervise their operation [21].

Intrusion detection systems are a fundamental component in the security process of every organization. These systems could produce a great number of data and some of them do not show the existing relationships between the reported alerts.

Traditionally, computer attacks were described in terms of a single vulnerability but complex attacks involve a series of actions before the attacker can reach his objectives [20]. It is important to analyze security alerts within their overall context, including related events occurring within the same timeframe [4].

Alert correlation is a process that allows the security administrator to increase the understanding of a given attack. This technique provides a global view of what is happening in a system in a particular moment. To better understand security threats, it is necessary to do some correlation process on the reported alerts. There are several proposed correlation methods but we they can be organized in the following four categories: (1) based on similarity, which consists on the aggregation of alerts by the calculation of similarities between some of their attributes; (2) based on predefined attack scenarios, which construct attack scenarios by matching the reported alerts with some user predefined templates; (3) based on prerequisites and consequences, which construct attack scenarios by matching the consequence of an attack with the preconditions of another one; and (4) based on multiple sources of information, which correlate alerts originated at different security systems [26]. These correlation methods have both advantages and disadvantages and we think that it is necessary an alternative solution that could be used by analysts in order to find relationships between the reported alerts without requiring the user to previously define the attack sequences that he expects to find.

6.3   Previous Works

Alert correlation can help to extract strategies from different reported intrusions and infer the attacker's main objectives [27]. There are various works that focus on the study of alert correlation. Valdes and Skinner presented a correlation method based on probabilities to find relationships between the reported alerts [23]. *LAMBDA* allows the user to specify attack scenarios, but it is restrained to known situations [27]. *JIGSAW* is a tool that allows the user to describe the components of a particular attack in terms of capabilities and concepts [20]. *TIAA* is another tool that helps the user to describe the prerequisites and consequences of individual attacks and then to correlate the detected attacks based on the relationships between the prerequisites of an attack with the consequences of another one. A prerequisite of an attack corresponds to the necessary conditions that need to be satisfied in order for a later attack to be successful, while the consequence of an attack is the obtained result after the attack was done [15]. Another correlation tool is *SEC*, which uses an approach based on user predefined rules [22]. Chyssler *et al* [3] proposed an alert correlation method based on neural nets. Also, there has been proposed a correlation method for logs that originate at different sources based on the concept of logical clocks [5].

Visualization of security information is a technique that helps the security administrator to better understand network usage [21].

VISALERT is a visual alert correlation tool that is based on the "*What, when and where*" attributes of the reported alerts [12]. *STARMINE* is a visualization system for monitoring attacks and that can show the relationships between the geographic and cybernetic spaces [7]. *SnortView* is a tool used to analyze the data reported by *Snort* and *syslog*, and then represents the reported alerts using different styled and colored icons [9].

In this work we use graphs to represent the reported alerts and show the relationships between. These graphs are generated using the concept of vector clocks. We propose a correlation model that allows the user to discover the sequences of a complex attack. With the used of this model it is no longer necessary to specify any kind of previous information in order to find the relationships between the analyzed alerts.

6.4   Vector Clocks

In 1978, Lamport presented the concept of logical clocks. Logical clocks can help us to order the events that occurred in a distributed environment and therefore give us an approximation of the real time in which those events occurred. In contrast to real time whose value changes independently of any event, logical time does not change its value by its own. A logical clock changes its value only when a new event occurs [11]. When we use logical time we need to assign a timestamp t to each event e, and we must meet the following two rules:

1. If an event e happens before another event e' inside the same process, then the timestamp assigned to event e is less than the one assigned to event e'.
2. For every message sent from one process to another, the timestamp of the sending event is less than the one assigned to the receipt event.

Logical clocks can be implemented assigning a counting system C_i to each process P_i, and the previous two conditions of logical time are satisfied with the following operations:

1. When process P_i executes an internal event or sends a message to another process, then its logical clock C_i is incremented with the following operation:

$$C_i = C_i + d (d > 0)$$

2. When process P_i receives a message (which also contains a timestamp), then its logical clock is incremented by the following operation:

$$C_i = max\,(C_i, t) + d\,(d > 0)$$

In general, the value of d is typically is 1 but it could be any other.

Lamport mentioned that those previous operations allow us to define the "*happened-before*" relationship, which states the following conditions:

1. $a \to b$, if a and b are events that happen inside the same process and a happened before b in time.
2. $a \to b$, if a corresponds to the event of sending a message m by one process and b is the event of the reception of that same message by another process.
3. If $a \to b$ and $b \to c$, then $a \to c$ (transitivity).
4. Event a causally precedes event b if: $a \to b$.
5. Two events a and b are concurrent to each other $(a \parallel b)$ if: $\neg(a \to b)$ && $\neg(b \to a)$.
6. For every two events a and b we have: $(a \to b)$, $(b \to a)$ or $(a \parallel b)$.

Mattern said that the mechanism proposed by Lamport could lose causality information, and the reason of this is because the events that happened simultaneously could be assigned different timestamps and this situation could seem that they occurred in a predefined order [13]. That is why he defined the concept of vector clocks, which is based on the concept of Lamport's logical clocks. In vector clocks, a clock C_i, which consists on a vector of integers of size n, is assigned to each process P_i. The value of n is equal to the number of different processes present in the system [13].

1. When process P_i executes and internal event or an event that corresponds to the sending of a message to another process, then it increases its local clock C_i with the following operation:

$$C_i = C_i\,[i] + d\,(d > 0)$$

2. When process P_i receives a message (which also includes a timestamp t), then its local clock is incremented with the following operation:

$$C_i[k] = max(C_i[k],\ t[k]), \text{where } k=1, 2, \ ..., n.$$

When a process receives a message, its local clock is updated in such a way that each component of its vector clock has the greatest value between the sender and the receiver. This way, vector clocks provide a mechanism that allows us to order the reported events and determine causality relationships between two given events simply by observing their timestamps [13].

It is possible to compare the timestamps of two events and determine if an event causally precedes the other or not, or if they are concurrent. This could be done with the following comparisons on two given vector clocks:

1. Two vector clock C_a and C_b are equal, $C_a = C_b$, if: $C_a[k] = C_b[k]$, where $k = 1, 2, ..., n$.
2. The vector clock of event a (C_a) is less than or equal to the vector clock of event b (C_b), $C_a \le C_b$, if: $C_a[k] \le C_b[k]$, where $k = 1, 2, ..., n$.

3. The vector clock of event a (C_a) is less than the vector clock of event b (C_b), $C_a < C_b$, if: $C_a \leq C_b$ and C_a is not equal to C_b.
4. Event a causally precedes event b, $a \to b$, if and only if: $C_a < C_b$.
5. Two events a and b are concurrent between each other, $C_a \parallel C_b$, if: $\neg(C_a < C_b)$ && $\neg(C_b < C_a)$.

6.5   Alert Correlation Model Based on Vector Clocks

In this paper we propose an alert correlation model based on the concept of vector clocks that allows us to find the relationships between the reported events and create graphs that show that information. We decided to use the concept of vector clocks and not Lamport's logical clocks because as we saw in the previous section, although Lamport's logical clocks allows us to determine which events happened before another one, they do not allows us to determine if they are causally related or not. For instance, if event a happened before event b, then we know that the timestamp of event a is less than the timestamp of event b, that is: If $a \to b$ then $C_a < C_b$, but if the timestamp of event a is less than the timestamp of event b, we can not know for sure if a causally precedes b or not, that is: If $C_a < C_b$, then $\neg(b \to a)$.

Figure 6.1 is an example that shows the concept of Lamport's logical clocks [13]. In this graph we can see that event $e_{1.1}$ has a timestamp with a value less than the value assigned to event $e_{3.2}$. We can see that these events are not related between each other since there does not exist a connected path between them.

Figure 6.2 represents the same example as the one in Figure 6.1 but in this graph we used the concept of vector clocks. In this figure we can see that event $e_{1.1}$ does not causally precede event $e_{3.2}$ and this is because the timestamp of event $e_{1.1}$ is not less than the timestamp of event $e_{3.2}$. One of the main characteristics of vector clocks is that their size is fixed, so we need to specify what kind of information is going to be represented by each component of the vectors in order to determine their size. In this correlation model we propose that each component of the vector clocks represent a distinct *IP* address of the reported alerts. We need to create a number of vector clocks equal to the number of different *IP* address and their size must be of the same value. For instance, if we find n unique *IP* addresses, then we create n vector clocks whose size is equal to n. For each of the reported alerts we generate two events, one that is the "*send*" of the attack by the source and the other that is the "*reception*" of that same attack.

6.5.1   Example of the Correlation Model

In order to demonstrate the functioning of our correlation model, we present the following example, in which the following alerts are reported:

Fig. 6.1 Example of Lamport's logical clocks

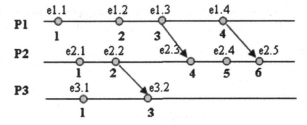

Fig. 6.2 Example of vector clocks

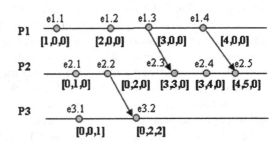

Fig. 6.3 Values assigned to the vector clocks based on the reported alerts

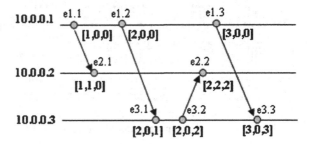

1. Aug 18 12:00:01 IDS13/portmap-request-mountd: 10.0.0.1 -> 10.0.0.2
2. Aug 18 12:01:01 IDS/DNS-version-query: 10.0.0.1 -> 10.0.0.3
3. Aug 18 12:03:01 IDS13/portmap-request-mountd: 10.0.0.3 -> 10.0.0.2
4. Aug 18 12:05:01 IDS159/Ping Microsoft Windows: 10.0.0.1 -> 10.0.0.3

In these four alerts we can see that there are a total of three distinct *IP* addresses, so we create three vector clocks of size three. Then, based on the information of the reported alerts, we calculate the value of each vector using the update operations of the vector clocks that we saw in section 6.4.

Figure 6.3 shows the values of the vector clocks assigned to each event. In this picture we can see that event $e_{1,2}$ (which corresponds to the sending of the attack *IDS/DNS-version-query* from the host 10.0.0.1 to 10.0.0.3) and $e_{2,1}$ (which corresponds to the reception of that same attack) are concurrent to each other and this is because $\neg(C_{e1,2} < C_{e2,1})$ && $\neg(C_{e2,1} < C_{e1,2})$. Also we can see that event $e_{3,3}$ is related to events $e_{1,3}$ and $e_{3,2}$. We also can know that events $e_{1,3}$ and $e_{3,3}$ are concurrent with respect to event $e_{2,2}$.

Using this information we can create the sequences of the events using its predecessors, which are those events for which there exists a direct path in the graph.

6.6   VALI

VALI (*Visual Analysis of Log Information*) is our implementation of the correlation model proposed in this paper. *VALI* is a tool that allows the user to generate graphs showing the relationships between the reported alerts. This tool allows the user to discover complex attacks. The produced graphs present the information in a simpler way than if they were analyzed in text files. *VALI* allows the user to create two types of graphs: a *detailed graph* that shows all of the reported alerts and the order in which they appeared; and a *reduced graph* that presents a higher level view of the reported alerts and that only shows the distinct alerts and their sequences.

Figure 6.4 shows an example of the output generated by an *IDS* and figures 6.5 and 6 correspond to segments of the detailed and reduced graphs, respectively.

In order to correlate the reported alerts, *VALI* follows these steps:

```
[**] [1:100000160:2] COMMUNITY SIP TCP/IP message flooding directed to SIP proxy [**]
[classification: Attempted Denial of Service] [Priority: 2]
03/07-08:21:56.071435 0:10:5A:9C:B2:8E -> 8:0:20:89:BA:28 type:0x800 len:0x71
172.16.112.100:1143 -> 172.16.115.20:53 UDP TTL:127 TOS:0x0 ID:14594 IpLen:20 DgmLen:99
Len: 71

[**] [1:100000160:2] COMMUNITY SIP TCP/IP message flooding directed to SIP proxy [**]
[classification: Attempted Denial of Service] [Priority: 2]
03/07-08:22:02.869452 8:0:20:89:BA:28 -> 0:10:5A:9C:B2:54 type:0x800 len:0xB1
172.16.115.20:53 -> 172.16.112.100:1234 UDP TTL:255 TOS:0x0 ID:20814 IpLen:20 DgmLen:163 DF
Len: 135

[**] [1:100000161:2] COMMUNITY SIP DNS No such name treshold - Abnormally high count of No such name responses [**]
[classification: Attempted Denial of Service] [Priority: 2]
03/07-08:22:54.581516 8:0:20:89:BA:28 -> 0:10:5A:9C:B2:54 type:0x800 len:0xAD
172.16.115.20:53 -> 172.16.112.100:1899 UDP TTL:255 TOS:0x0 ID:21921 IpLen:20 DgmLen:159 DF
Len: 131
```

Fig. 6.4 Example of the output generated by an *IDS* in text format

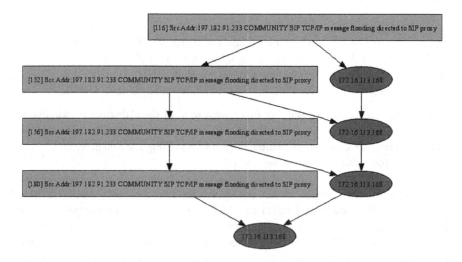

Fig. 6.5 Segment of a detailed graph generated using *VALI* that represents some of the reported data

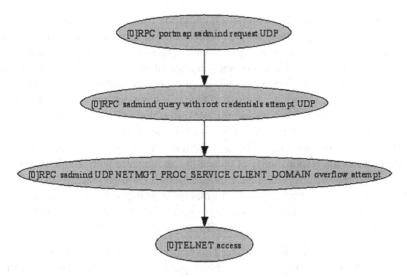

Fig. 6.6 Example of a reduced graph generated using *VALI*

1. It identifies the distinct *IP* addresses in all of the reported alerts.
2. It creates the different vector clocks, whose sizes are equal to the number of distinct *IP* address found in step 1.
3. For each of the reported alerts, it identifies the source and destination addresses, and then creates two events: one that corresponds to the *"sending"* of the attack and the other that represents the *"reception"* of that attack.
4. In order to determine which events are interrelated, *VALI* applies the rules of vector clocks. We must remember that this mechanism allows us to determine if two events are concurrent or one is the predecessor of the other.
5. Finally, it creates the graphs that show the reported alerts and the connections between them.

6.6.1 VALI Components

VALI was developed using the *Java* programming language and is comprised of the following four parts:

1. Alert preprocessing
2. Correlation engine
3. Graph generation
4. Graphical user interface

The alert preprocessing component takes as input the information corresponding to the reported alerts. This information is originally stored in text files, so this component is responsible for parsing the data in order to get the necessary information for the correlation process. The correlation engine is based on the concept of vector clocks. This component analyzes the preprocessed information and finds the existing relationships between the reported events. Once the alerts have been correlated, it is necessary to present this information in a way that is easy to analyze and understand. We think that a graph is a convenient representation because it provides a simpler view of the reported information than if it were presented in text format. In order to create these graphs, we use the *dot* utility that is included in the *GraphViz* package [6]. We use *dot* because it is a useful and flexible tool and allows us to generate simple directed graphs. Finally, we have the graphical user interface component that has the responsibility of presenting an interface with which the user can interact with the system. When the user generates a detailed graph of the information, he can specify which type of information is going to be included in each of the nodes of the graph. The user is able to specify different parameters that control how the graph is going to be produced. These parameters are:

1. Information included in each node. This option allows the user to specify which type of information is going to be shown per node. The information that can be displayed could be the following: IP address, date, hour, and alert description.
2. Assign geometric shapes to specific data. The user can assign different geometric shapes to nodes that represent a particular type of information. With this feature, the user can distinguish more rapidly the type of information that most interests him.

This configuration data is stored in *XML* files and for its manipulation we use the *Java JAXP API*.

Figure 6.7 shows some of the main windows of the *VALI* graphic user interface. In this picture we can distinguish the following four components: a table of the reported alerts; a history of the generated graphs corresponding to the reported data; a segment of a detailed graph generated with *VALI*; and the main window.

6.7   Experiments and Results

In order to evaluate the effectiveness of our proposed correlation mechanism we made some experiments using the *MIT Lincoln Laboratory's DARPA Intrusion Detection Evaluation 2000* dataset [14]. This dataset corresponds to an attack whose premise is that an adversary uses a script to gain access to a number of hosts. After the attacker has successfully gained access to the compromised systems he installs the necessary components that will permit him to launch a distributed denial of service attack (*DDoS*) and finally execute a *DDoS* against a US internet government site. The attacker exploits a vulnerability of the *sadmind* remote administration service for *Solaris* systems. This exploit will permit the attacker to gain *root* access to three *Solaris* hosts. The adversary uses the *MStream DDoS* tool, which has two main components: an *MStream server* that is installed in each of the victims and that is responsible to generate and send packets for the *DDoS*; and an *MStream*

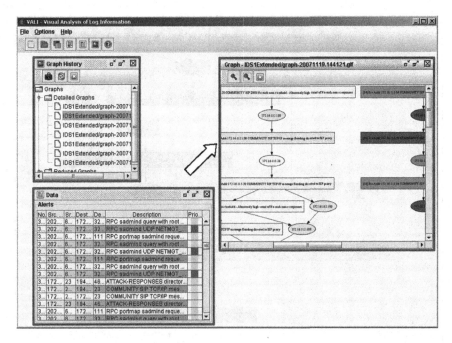

Fig. 6.7   *VALI* graphic user interface

master that is only installed in one of the victims and presents a user interface with which the attacker can interact and launch the *DDoS*. The attack is divided in five different phases.

In phase 1 the attacker sends *ICMP echo-requests* to determine which hosts are active and connected to the network. In phase 2 the attacker determines which of the active hosts found in phase 1 are running the *sadmind* service and possibly vulnerable to the attack. In phase 3 the attacker uses the attack script, which in turn tries to do many *Remote-to-Root* exploits to the *sadmind* service. To determine if the attack succeeded, the attacker tries to login into the host. In phase 4 the script has already created a list of all the hosts in which the attack was successful and that are ready to obey the orders from the *MStream master*. Finally, in phase 5 the adversary logins into the victim in which the *MStream master* was installed and from there he executes the command that launches the *DDoS*.

We analyzed this attack using *Snort* [17]. *Snort* reported us a total of 1,515 alerts in text files. We used this information as input for the *VALI* tool. At the time of this writing the only input that *VALI* accepts is the one generated by Snort, but it is possible to extend the tool in order to process information generated by another *IDS*. *VALI* allowed us to create a detailed graph that showed us the reported alerts and how they were related. We also created a reduced graph that showed us the distinct alert types and how they were related. Figure 6.8 corresponds to a segment of the detailed graph generated with *VALI*. In this graph we can see some of the reported alerts, the order in which they appeared and how they were interrelated.

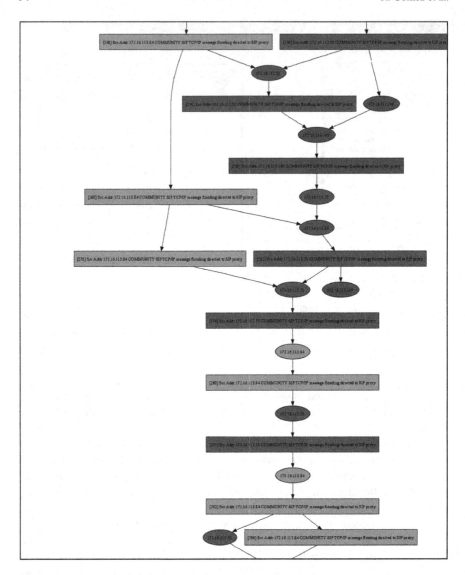

Fig. 6.8 Segment of a detailed graph generated with the data of the experiment

Figure 6.9 corresponds to the reduced graph generated with *VALI*, which is more general than the detailed graph presented in Figure 6.8. This reduced graph does not show us all of the detailed data of every reported alert but only the distinct reported alerts and how they are interrelated.

As we can see from the generated graphs, these experiments allowed us to demonstrate how *VALI* correctly represented the information of the attack described in the different phases without losing any of the sequences in which they appeared.

It is important to mention that in order to find the relationships between the reported alerts we did not have to specify any kind of information related to the attack. The total

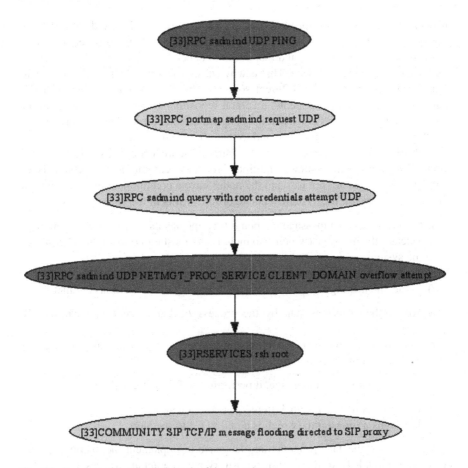

Fig. 6.9 Segment of the detailed graph of the experiment

of more than one thousand alerts were successfully correlated helped us to trace the attack pattern from the ping commands to the exploit against the systems.

We consider that one of the main advantages of this correlation model is that it is not necessary to indicate any information regarding to the sequences of complex attacks, therefore we reduce the likelihood of not finding a complex attack for which we do not have information. Another advantage of this tool is that the user does not have to analyze thousands of alerts that are originally contained in text files.

6.8   Distributed Alert Correlation Model

In the previous sections, we showed how vector clocks can be used to correlate security information and extract attack strategies from raw alerts. However, the process of determining which event happened before another given event could be difficult if the alerts were produced at different sources and they do not share a global clock. Therefore, it is necessary to have a mechanism to order the alerts produced at different sources and that does not depend solely on the clocks configured in each machine or device. That is why we also developed a model to correlate security alerts originated at different sources. This distributed correlation model consists of two main components: a central repository that receives and stores all of the generated alerts, and also a number of agents that are responsible for broadcasting the alerts to the central repository and to the other agents in the system.

In this correlation model we used the Birman-Schiper-Stephenson (BSS) algorithm. This algorithm assumes multiple broadcast communication channels in which the messages are not lost and the nodes have a communication channel with all the other nodes in the system. This algorithm works in the following manner:

1. If process P_i sends a message m, then it first updates its vector clock C_i and then broadcasts the message (which also includes a timestamp t) to all the other nodes in the system.
2. When process $P_j \neg (j = i)$ receives a message m (which also includes the timestamp t), it puts the message in a stack until the following two conditions are met:

   a. All of the messages sent by the process P_i that precede m have already arrived.
   b. The process P_j has received all the messages that process P_i has also received before sending message m.
3. When an agent sends a message, it performs the following actions:

   a. It increases its vector clock in its own component.
   b. It assigns a timestamp (which is equal to C_i) to the alert.

We also used the Java programming language to implement the distributed alert correlation model. Both the central repository and the agents are responsible for the reception of messages and the sorting of those messages so that they preserve the correct order in which the messages were generated. This responsibility is very important because we do not have to rely anymore on the value of the timestamp assigned to the messages by the computers or devices in which they were generated.

For instance, if the central repository receives this two alerts:

1. Server received message: VectorClockUpdate (1)[0,2,1]<13>Feb 29 11:31:16 SEC1 MSWinEventLog<009>...
2. Server received message: VectorClockUpdate (0)[1,2,1]<13>Feb 29 02:52:56 SEC2 MSWinEventLog<009>...

Then, instead of focusing on the timestamps given by the local clocks of the computers at which those alerts were generated (which are 11:31:16 for the first alert, and 02:52:56 for the second one), we can compare the timestamps calculated by the vector clocks (which are [0,2,1] for the first alert, and [1,2,1] for the second one). In this particular example, we can see that alert 2 has a timestamp whose value is less than the one of alert 1.

The central repository and the agents can be installed in computers with different clocks. Neither the central repository nor the agents are responsible for generating security alerts, their sole responsibility is to share the security information between them and sort it in the correct way in which they were produced.

In this distributed alert correlation model, the central repository is responsible for receiving the messages from the agents, sort them in the correct order in which they were generated and storing them for latter retrieval. That way, when a user consults the alerts stored at the central repository, he could be certain that the alerts are in the correct order, despite the timestamp assigned by the local machine.

6.9   Conclusions and Future Work

It is important to have at our disposal different tools that help us to discover or prevent attacks targeted to our systems. Current attacks are complex and involve various activities with the objective of getting information or tearing down systems. There are many tools that generate alerts when they identify a potential attack. Although the information produced by these systems is valuable, the number of generated alerts could be huge and therefore difficult to analyze. We also have to consider that this information is generally stored in text format. In order to extract attack patterns from this information we have to parse the reported alerts and try to find relationships between them.

In this paper we presented an alert correlation model based on the concept of vector clocks. We also presented *VALI* which is our own implementation of the correlation model. This tool can be used by security analysts to produce graphs in order to present the information in a visual format. VALI not only relieves the user from analyzing text files but also allows him to discover the existing relationships between the reported alerts in simple way. Although the correlation model presented in this paper is not the solution to all of the needs of security analysts, we think that it can be used to discover and identify the different activities that comprise a complex attack and therefore to have a global view of what is happening to their systems. This visual representation replaces the need of focusing on hundreds or thousands of individual alerts that could originally seem to be unrelated.

We also presented a distributed alert correlation model that used the concept of vector clocks to correlate information generated at different sources so we no longer have to depend on a global synchronized clock for the analysis of information.

References

1. Bejtlich R (2005) The Tao of Network Security Monitoring. Beyond Intrusion Detection. Addison-Wesley, U.S.A.
2. Casey E (2006) Investigating Sophisticated Security Breaches. Communications of the ACM. Vol. 49. No. 2. U.S.A.

3. Chyssler T et al (2004) Alarm Reduction and Correlation in Defense of IP Networks. Proceedings of the 13th IEEE International Workshops on Enabling Technologies: Infrastructure for Collaborative Enterprises, WET ICE'04
4. Goodall J et al (2005) A User-Centered Approach to Visualizing Network Traffic for Intrusion Detection. Extended Abstracts of the ACM Conference on Human Factors in Computing Systems (CHI). ACM Press, 1403–1406. U.S.A.
5. Gomez R, Herrerias J, Mata E (2006) Using Lamport's logical clocks to consolidate log files from different sources. Lecture Notes in Computer Science. Innovative Internet Community Systems. Springer Berlin Heidelberg. Vol. 3908/2006. 126–133
6. Graphviz - Graph Visualization Software, http://www.graphviz.org
7. Hideshima Y, Koike H (2006) STARMINE: A Visualization System for Cyber Attacks. Proceedings of the Asia Pacific symposium on Information visualization – Vol. 60. Australian Computer Society Inc., Australia
8. Jha S, Sheyner O, Wing J (2002) Two Formal Analyses of Attack Graphs. Proceedings of the 15th Computer Security Foundation Workshop IEEE. 49–63. U.S.A.
9. Koike H, Ohno K (2004) SnortView: Visualization System of Snort Logs. Proceedings of the 2004 ACM workshop on Visualization and data mining for computer security VizSEC/DMSEC'04. ACM Press. U.S.A.
10. Komlodi A, Goodall J, Lutters W (2004) An Information Visualization Framework for Intrusion Detection. CHI'04 extended abstracts on Human factors in computing systems CHI'04. ACM Press. 1743. U.S.A.
11. Lamport L (1978) Time, Clocks, and the Ordering of Events in a Distributed System. Communications of the ACM. Vol. 21, No. 7. U.S.A.
12. Livnat Y, et al (2005) A Visualization Paradigm for Network Intrusion Detection. Proceedings of the 2005 IEEE workshop on Information Assurance and Security. United States Military Academy, West Point. NY, U.S.A.
13. Mattern F (1988) Virtual Time and Global States of Distributed Systems. Proceedings of the International workshop on Parallel and Distributed Algorithms. Elsevier Science Publishers. 215–226. Holland
14. MIT Lincoln Laboratory – DARPA Intrusion Detection Evaluation Documentation, http://www.ll.mit.edu/IST/ideval/docs/docs_index.html
15. Ning P, et al (2004) Techniques and Tools for Analyzing Intrusion Alerts. ACM Transactions on Information and System Security (TISSEC). Vol. 7. Issue 2. 274–318. ACM Press, U.S.A.
16. Raynal M (1992) About logical clocks for distributed systems. ACM SIGOPS Operating Systems Review. Vol. 26. Issue 1. 41–48. ACM Press, U.S.A.
17. Snort – the de facto standard for intrusion detection/prevention, http://www.snort.org
18. Sun C, Cai W (2002) Capturing Causality by Compressed Vector Clock in Real-time Group Editors. Parallel and Distributed Processing Symposium. Proceedings International, IPDPS. 59–66. IEEE Computer Society. U.S.A.
19. Tannenbaum A, van Steen M (2007) Distributed Systems. Principles and Paradigms. Pearson Prentice Hall. U.S.A.
20. Templeton S, Levitt K (2001) A Requires/Provides Model for Computer Attacks. Proceedings of the 2000 workshop on new security paradigms. 31–38. ACM Press. U.S.A.
21. Tölle J, Niggemann O (2002) Supporting Intrusion Detection by Graph Clustering and Graph Drawing. Proceedings of the 3rd International workshop on Recent advances in Intrusion Detection
22. Vaarandi R (2002) SEC – A lightweight Event Correlation Tool. IEEE Workshop on IP Operations and Management IPOM. 111–115 IEEE
23. Valdes A, Skinner K (2001) Probabilistic Alert Correlation. Lecture Notes In Computer Science Vol. 2212. Proceedings of the 14th International Symposium on Recent Advances in Intrusion Detection. Springer-Verlang. 54–68. England
24. Viinikka J, et al (2006) Time Series Modeling for IDS Alert Management. Proceedings of the 2006 ACM Symposium on Information, computer and communications security. 102–113. ACM Press. U.S.A.

25. Xu D, Ning P (2005) Privacy-Preserving Alert Correlation: A Concept Hierarchy Based Approach. 21st Computer Security Applications Conference
26. Zhu B, Ghorbani A (2006) Alert Correlation for Extracting Attack Strategies. International Journal of Network Security, Vol. 3, No. 3, 244–258
27. Zurutuza U, Uribeetxeberria R (2004) Intrusion Detection Alarm Correlation: A Survey. Proceedings of the IADAT International Conference on Telecommunications and Computer Networks

Chapter 7
An Open Architecture for Distributed Malware Collection and Analysis

Davide Cavalca and Emanuele Goldoni

Abstract Honeynets have become an important tool for researchers and network operators. However, the lack of a unified honeynet data model has impeded their effectiveness, resulting in multiple unrelated data sources, each with its own proprietary access method and format. Moreover, the deployment and management of a honeynet is a time-consuming activity and the interpretation of collected data is far from trivial. HIVE (Honeynet Infrastructure in Virtualized Environment) is a novel highly scalable automated data collection and analysis architecture we designed. Our infrastructure is based on top of proven FLOSS (Free, Libre and Open Source) solutions, which have been extended and integrated with new tools we developed. We use virtualization to ease honeypot management and deployment, combining both high-interaction and low-interaction sensors in a common infrastructure. We also address the need for rapid comprehension and detailed data analysis by harnessing the power of a relational database system, which provides centralized storage and access to the collected data while ensuring its constant integrity. This chapter presents our malware data collection architecture, offering some insight in the structure and benefits of a distributed virtualized honeynet and its development. Finally, we present some techniques for the active monitoring of centralized botnets we integrated in HIVE, which allow us to track the menaces evolution and timely deploy effective countermeasures.

7.1 Introduction

In last years there has been a dramatic increase in malware activity on the Internet: according to [41], the last two years saw a 1500% increase in threat volume, with major contributions from botnet creation and expansion. To identify, prevent and

D. Cavalca (✉)
Department of Computer Engineering and Systems Science, University of Pavia, Pavia, Italy
e-mail: davide.cavalca01@ateneopv.it

E. Goldoni
Department of Electronics, University of Pavia, Pavia, Italy
e-mail: emanuele.goldoni@unipv.it

E. Huebner and S. Zanero (eds.), *Open Source Software for Digital Forensics*,
DOI 10.1007/978-1-4419-5803-7_7, © Springer Science+Business Media, LLC 2010

actively counteract the impeding menaces it's important to maintain a constant monitoring of criminal activity on the network. To be able to successfully defend itself, every networked company has to carry the burden of threat monitoring, building and maintaining a dedicated infrastructure. Due to the recent shift from mass attacks (mostly represented by viruses) to targeted attacks, which are performed for a specific purpose (data theft, disruption of operations, etc.), threat control has become even more compelling.

Thanks to The Honeynet Project [2] and similar initiatives, the employment of honeypots for threat monitoring has grown into wide usage. There are now several honeynets monitoring the Internet, deployed both by academic and commercial organizations, for research and defense purposes. Most of these honeynets are independent and disconnected: they are owned and maintained by a single organization and they serve a specific purpose; the data they collect is often kept confidential, especially for commercial organizations. Moreover, each and every honeynet uses a different, generally homegrown, data collection and analysis system, impairing interoperability with external systems. Even if a company *wants* to share its honeynet data, it is often difficult to integrate different data sources in a unified system. The mwcollect Alliance [4] has taken a step in the right direction, building a single infrastructure for the collection of honeynet data and the monitoring of threats in a collaborative fashion. But the Alliance is a centralized system, essentially closed, for safety reasons: there is no public information on their infrastructure. The same can be said for the Leurrecom project [3]: the data acquired from their infrastructure is not publicly available and access is bound to a Non-Disclosure Agreement. Their software, while being based on Open Source technologies, is not developed in collaboration with the Open Source community and is only distributed to entities hosting at least one Leurrecom honeypot sensor.

We believe there is a need for an open honeynet infrastructure, to lower the barrier required to setup and operate an honeypot network and to ease data collection and analysis. The openness needs to be both structural and material: open and common data schemas make the sharing of information effortless, thus encouraging it. Honeypot data based on open formats is easier to access, process and preserve, thus being better suited to serve research purposes. On the other hand, the use of Open Source software to implement the actual infrastructure makes it easy for everyone to study, build, audit and improve it, allowing the whole community to benefit from individual efforts. The commitment of commercial entities to an open honeynet framework would empower the research community and greatly benefit the industry to improve the understanding of Internet threats and the development of timely countermeasures.

The remainder of this chapter is organized as follows: in Section 2 we discuss previous works in this area and its relation with our research. The architecture and implementation of HIVE (Honeynet Infrastructure in Virtualized Environment), our proposed honeynet infrastructure, is described in detail in Section 3. We present some results from our testbed system in Section 4. Finally, in Section 5 we conclude and lay out the grounds for some future works.

7.2   Background and Related Work

The use of honeypots for malware detection and capture is now a well established field. Two major kinds of honeypots have been developed: low interaction honeypots simulate vulnerable services or environments to lure malware into attacking them and capture its sample. They are easy to deploy and require low maintenance, but the simulation is imperfect and they can often be detected or circumvented [17, 23]. Notable Open Source projects in this area are Honeyd [29], Nepenthes [6] and HoneyTrap [42]; a recent research contribution, still in heavy development, is Amun [12] which is significantly easier to extend that its predecessors, due to a novel modular approach. High interaction honeypots, on the other hand, use a full-edged system as a bait; the honeypot machine is periodically analyzed, malware is collected and the system is rebuilt to a clean state. This kind of honeypot can potentially capture many more malware samples, but is also much more expensive to deploy and maintain. Nowadays, high interaction honeypots are often implemented using virtualization, which eases most of their drawbacks but potentially makes them easier to detect and thus vulnerable to targeted attacks [17, 46].

There is sizable body of research on low-interaction systems, while high interaction honeynets have historically received less attention. The creation of low interaction systems has required the development of a theoretical framework to analyze and model the object of simulation; nowadays, this kind of honeypots is widely used, being lightweight and easy to deploy. On the other hand, high-interaction systems require a larger upfront investment | readymade systems are scarce, have a larger footprint and are much less polished. There are also legal liability concerns: it is necessary to avoid that a compromised high interaction honeypot takes part in a potentially dangerous attack to external machines (e.g. a denial of service).

The HoneyBow project [45] deployed a sensor infrastructure using virtualized VMware systems combined with Nepenthes [6] sensors to capture malware samples. While part of the software they developed is freely available at [35], it has not received any significant update in the last two years. The HoneyBow project also fails to detail their data storage and analysis system, focusing instead on the collection infrastructure and the analysis of collected data. A similar approach is employed by the Leurrecom Project [20], which combines VMware and Honeyd [29] to gather data for a private centralized collection system.

In [30] Rajab et al. developed a botnet measurement infrastructure using Nepenthes sensors and a physical honeynet. They focused on IRC bots, developing a series of tools to study and infiltrate these kinds of botnets. While they make the collected data available to the research community, to our knowledge the developed software has not been released.

Colajanni et al. present in [10] a multi-tier architecture for malware collection and analysis, based on Nephentes sensors managed by Prelude [5]; their work, still in heavy development, is mainly focused on the deployment of active countermeasures to the detected menaces.

7.3   Implementation of HIVE

We chose to structure HIVE on a three-tier architecture, shown in Fig. 7.1, to fully decouple data acquisition from data memorization. This decision has a twofold advantage: it is easier to build and scale the whole system, and if a honeypot sensor is compromised there is no way it can harm (or even see) the data store.

The first stage is the actual honeynet, which is implemented using virtualization and features a combination of low-interaction and high-interaction sensors. Malware samples acquired from the honeypots are sent to a *gateway*, which validates and preprocesses them. Samples then flow to the data store, where they are permanently stored and analysis is performed. Malware samples are analyzed with the help of external services, which provide reports on the samples' behavior to help classification. Monitoring facilities query the data store to obtain threat information (e.g. botnet controller servers' addresses) and oversee their evolution.

The architecture is fully scalable: adding more sensors is only a matter of creating new virtual machines or adding other physical systems. If a honeypot is damaged or compromised, it cannot affect other sensors and it can be easily rebuilt or replaced. Structure and implementation of the honeynet and its sensors is described in Section 3.1. The gateway (which itself can be replicated with no effort) allows preliminary filtering of honeypot data: we can potentially remove bogus samples before sending them to the data store, avoiding to waste system resources on their analysis. The data store, finally, can be made redundant using database replication, and itself relies on multiple providers to perform the samples' analysis, to achieve better accuracy and lower the samples turnaround. This part of HIVE, which can be considered its core, is presented in Section 3.2.

7.3.1 Honeynet Sensors

We chose to implement our honeypot sensors using virtualization. As noted before in [45], virtualization dramatically cuts down the efforts needed to deploy

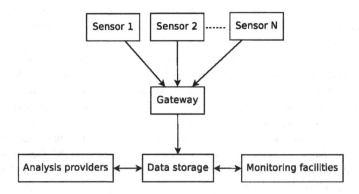

Fig. 7.1 Block diagram of HIVE architecture

and manage the honeynet. Moreover, the ability to simulate an arbitrary network topology on a single physical machine allows us to dynamically reconfigure the honeynet. This choice is not mandatory: our infrastructure works equally well with virtual and physical honeypots, but in the latter case deploying the sensor and periodically restoring the honeypot to a clean state will require considerably more efforts.

We based our implementation on VirtualBox [33], an Open Source virtualization product. VirtualBox has similar performance to its more prominent competitor VMware, which has been used in honeypot research [45, 20], is multi-platform and features some advantages from our point of view. Besides being Open Source, it's fully scriptable using a command-line interface, allowing us to easily automate the honeypots management operations using a few shell scripts. Compared to Xen, another leading Open Source virtualization product, VirtualBox does not require dedicated hardware support to execute unmodified guests (such as Microsoft closed-source operating systems). Another solution is Argos [27], a modified QEMU x86 emulator [9], which uses dynamic taint analysis to detect attacks in network code. In our view, Argos is more suited to the study of attack vectors and exploits, rather than the collection and analysis of live malware samples, which is the focus of HIVE. Nevertheless, Argos sensors could be a valuable addition to a distributed honeynet, and we are evaluating its use in future works. Our back-end is product agnostic by design and is not tied to any particular choice.

We believe that using a combination of low-interaction and high-interaction honeypots allows us to get the best of both worlds; through the use of virtualization, we are able to nullify the traditional problems (difficult and expensive deployment and maintenance) associated with high-interaction systems. We are currently using Nepenthes [6] for the low interaction sensors and a Gen- III Windows honeynet [7] for the high-interaction. An HoneyWall [37] 'Roo' gateway, itself running in a VM (Virtual Machine), monitors incoming and outgoing traffic to the high interaction honeynet. It is important to limit outgoing traffic, to avoid being part of an attack or a denial-of-service and thus preserving legal liability [17].

The Windows honeypots are automatically rebuilt twice a day from a clean snapshot. Before the rebuild, their disk contents are analyzed: we register the differences with a clean installation and send to the gateway the new executables found – potential malware samples – for further analysis. The deployment and rebuilding of VMs is currently implemented with the VirtualBox command-line utility (*VBoxManage*). Our rebuild script works as follows:

1. power the VM off;
2. read-only mount the virtual disk on the host system;
3. compare the virtual disk directory tree to a clean image (using the standard Unix tool *diff*), logging any file added, modified or removed;
4. copy each and every *.exe* file added (potential malware) to a temporary collection directory;
5. submit the collected samples to the gateway with a properly formatted HTTP request (using a Python script);
6. unmount and remove the VM virtual disk;

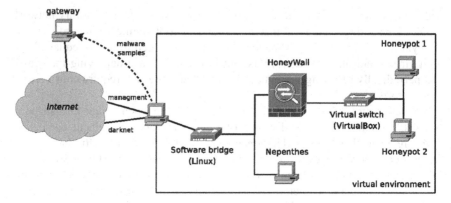

Fig. 7.2 Our virtual honeynet structure

7. clone the reference image into a new virtual disk (using the built-in VirtualBox cloning facility);
8. power on the VM, which is now ready for a new collection round.

We found this procedure to be the most reliable, although rather expensive (due to the use of the *diff* tool). Preliminary testing of client-based collection tools, such as MwWatcher and MwFetcher from the HoneyBow project [35], showed poor reliability and a large number of missed samples. We also tried Sebek [36], a kernel-space rootkit which monitors the honeypot activity (keyboard events, disk access, network usage) and reports to HoneyWall. In our tests, Sebek was extremely unstable, leading to frequent crashes of the honeypot operating systems. Finally, using the VirtualBox snapshotting features for the honeypot rebuild was not an option – snapshots are stored in a proprietary format and they cannot be easily mounted for analysis.

The honeynet structure is shown in Fig. 7.2. Linux software bridging [38] interconnects HoneyWall and the Nepenthes sensors with the darknet; the Windows honeypots are connected through a VirtualBox internal network (an isolated virtual switch) to HoneyWall internal interface.

7.3.2 Core Infrastructure

Once malware samples have been acquired, they must be processed, stored and analyzed. The life cycle of a malware sample in HIVE is shown in Fig. 7.3. The gateway exposes a web service to receive samples from the sensors; every sample has some metadata attached (file details, name of the sensor, date of collection and cryptographic hash). We have currently implemented the web service using a PHP script which receives data via HTTP POST.

A simplified version of the Entity-Relationship diagram for the database schema is shown in Fig. 7.4. We chose to rely on PostgreSQL 8.3, an Open Source object-relational DataBase Management System (DBMS): it supports most of the major

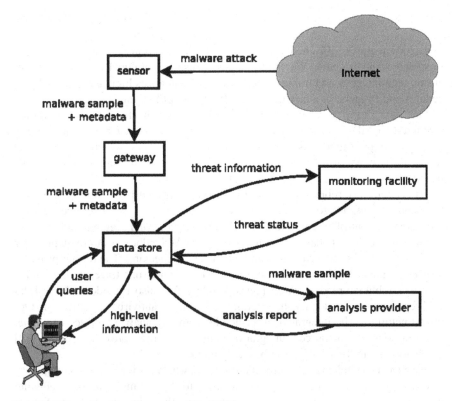

Fig. 7.3 Life cycle of a malware sample in HIVE

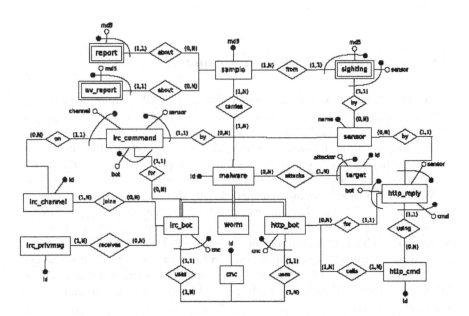

Fig. 7.4 Simplified Entity-Relationship diagram for HIVE database

SQL:2003 features [40], including referential integrity, transactions, views, stored procedures and triggers. We made extensive use of foreign keys constrains to ensure data integrity and implemented most of the analysis logic using stored procedures and triggers, in a mixture of pl/pgSQL and pl/Python.

Our data model is centered around *samples,* which are uniquely identified through their MD5 digest and stored in binary fields in the database. The addition of a new sample triggers its submission to external services, which analyze it and return a *report.* We use the collected reports to categorize the samples and extract useful data.

HIVE currently relies on the external services offered by Anubis [18, 8] and CWSandbox [34, 44] for the analysis of malware samples. Both services run the malware in a controlled environment, tracing its actions and logging network connections to provide a behavioral analysis. We use CWSandbox as our main provider and rely on Anubis for verification and human cross-checking. The former provides a machine-parsable XML report and a PCAP [22] network trace, while Anubis reports are human-readable web pages. CWSandbox also provides a VirusTotal [16] report we use to identify the malware according to antivirus classification. Our infrastructure can be integrated, in principle, with any analysis service available, either in-house or outsourced; integration with, for example, providers Joebox [19] and Norman SandBox [24] could be easily implemented.

We have also implemented a pre-filtering stage, which allows HIVE to preliminary screen the samples at gateway or analysis layer for known malware, thus reducing the load on external services. The analysis currently relies on the Open Source antivirus scanner ClamAV [32], but could be extended to support other antivirus engines.

7.3.3 Data Analysis and Active Monitoring

Our database schema currently accounts for IRC and HTTP centralized botnets and generic network worms. We make an extensive use of database views to aggregate data and present it in a coherent fashion. Views allow also to disclose useful data without compromising the necessary anonymity on the location of honeypot sensors and attack targets. We currently lack a full- edged reporting interface: data analysis is currently done directly querying the database.

We wrote a Google Maps mashup to graphically show the geographic distribution of botnet C&C (Command and Control) centers; the centers' IP addresses were geolocated using MaxMind GeoLite City [21]. This example shows how easy it is to access the collected data and mangle it in the needed way. As shown in Fig. 7.5, the control centers are spread worldwide in the areas of major Internet usage. A comparison with Fig. 7.6, which is a map of worldwide Internet infections during 2008 as detected by security firm F-Secure [1], shows a striking similarity with our results.

Fig. 7.5 Geographic distribution of the botnet C&Cs monitored by HIVE

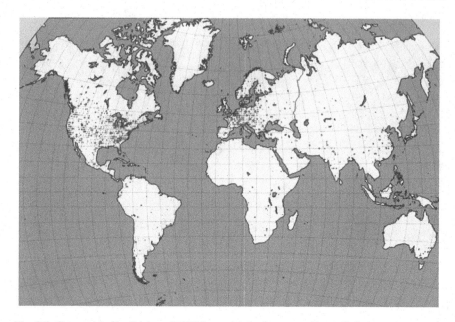

Fig. 7.6 Geographic distribution of 2008 Internet infections according to F-Secure

Using the data collected during analysis we have all the information needed to connect to the botnet C&C and impersonate a bot. To study IRC botnets, we extended the Infiltrator Open Source software [13] by Jan Göbel to interface with our database. Infiltrator connects to the C&C and logs every communication on the channel, providing insight in the botnet operations and targets. To achieve a similar analysis for HTTP botnets, we wrote httpmole, a Python program which periodically connects to the command center and reads its reply. Since the reply is arbitrary and different botnets use different ad hoc control software, some form of fingerprinting is needed to be able to parse these messages in a useful way. We are currently evaluating whether to pursue the development of httpmole or integrate our modifications with the latest Infiltrator release [14], which features basic HTTP botnet support.

7.3.4 Caveats and Pitfalls

The use of virtual machines for the honeypot implementation opens them to a risk (albeit small) of being detected. Virtualization detection is rather easy and several works have been published on this subject [17]; nevertheless, we are not aware of any widespread malware checking for a virtualized environment. As studied by [25], virtualization may pose a security risk: if an attacker is able to exploit a weakness in the VM software, he may be able to execute arbitrary code on the host system, potentially breaking into it. An automated periodic rebuild of the host systems would address this concern. On the other hand, the eventual compromise of honeypot sensors is not a catastrophic event: while the sensor could send bogus data, it has no way to directly access the database. In case of a suspect break-in, it is rather trivial to setup the gateway to ignore traffic from a specific sensor until the situation is investigated. The compromise of a sensor becomes problematic if the acquired data is directly used to deploy countermeasures: if the system is not well designed the attacker could be able to trigger a specific reaction, e.g. cutting off some portions of the network. For this reason, it is a good practice to employ data mining techniques to prescreen the data.

The strategic weakness of every honeypot is its secrecy: if an attacker were to discover the honeypot's address, he could blacklist it or send targeted attacks trying to disable, poison or subvert it. For this reason, it is mandatory to sanitize the collected data before publication [26]. As shown by [46], honeypots can potentially be detected by specially crafted malwares; refer to [11] for a HoneyWall targeted example. While there are no reports of current malware in the wild exploiting such techniques, this is a legitimate concern.

To extract meaningful statistics, it's important to have an even distribution of honeynets, both in geographical and in IP address space. In order to acquire a good understanding of Internet threats a very large number of sensors would be necessary. On the other hand, a global knowledge must be completed by a good understanding of local malicious activities – as shown by [28], it's essential to deploy geographically local sensors.

The critical point of HIVE is the database – the DBMS server represents a single point of failure of the infrastructure. This limitation can be overcome using replication techniques to duplicate it on multiple machines. Slony [39] is an Open Source replication system for PostgreSQL which could be useful for this purpose.

7.4   Experimental Results

We built a simple testbed system to evaluate HIVE feasibility. We used only two physical machines for simplicity: one ran the virtual honeynet, the other implemented the gateway and the data store. Our honeynet was composed of two Windows systems and a Nepenthes sensor, on a small darknet of three previously unused IP addresses on a commercial network. Previous experiments on an academic network proved unsuccessful, due to heavy filtering employed at the network borders (which stopped a large number of incoming attacks). Moreover, we observed that many attackers tend to avoid or blacklist the IP space of research organizations. We provisioned the high interaction honeypots with Windows 2000 Server and Windows XP Professional, both unpatched and with default configurations. A vast majority of malware targets these Microsoft systems: XP is probably the most widespread client system, while the presence of 2000 Server allows us to capture samples attacking server-grade services (such as IIS).

Fig. 7.7 Distribution of acquired samples by type

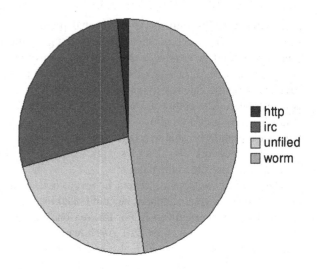

During a month of operation, we detected more than 14,000 malware samples (about 13,000 unique), classified as in Fig. 7.7. Looking at the big picture, it seems that HTTP bots are a negligible part, compared to other threats. The 'worm' samples – about a half of the total – are due to the Allaple polymorphic worm, which spreads through Microsoft systems using network share and buffer overflow vulnerabilities [31]. We actually found it difficult to relate the samples' cryptographic hashes with the different malware types, due to the use of these polymorphic techniques. This is, in our opinion, the reason for the small gap between the total and unique samples data. The 'unfiled' samples are currently not classified: they may be corrupt samples (which are screened but currently not included in results) or types of malware still unknown to our system or to the analysis services we rely on.

Fig. 7.8 shows the weekly samples breakdown by threat type. There has been a spike in the sixth week, due to a specific IRC bot, which spread over 2,000 samples on one honeypot, all tied to a single C&C center and with different hashes. Due to the strong locality of our sensors, the acquired data has a strong geographic bias and cannot be used to draw large scale conclusions in good faith.

In Fig. 7.9 and Fig. 7.10 we present the preliminary results from our monitoring infrastructure. We tracked about 50 different IRC botnets for two weeks, logging the activity on the control channel. The majority of botnet control is performed with private messages (PRIVMSG), and most commands issued are network scans and botnet expansion. There is a small but significant group of commands targeted at acquiring valuable data (credit card numbers, Internet games CD keys, passwords, etc.) from the infected systems, using primitive scanning techniques; in our view this is a serious menace to the privacy of networked organizations data.

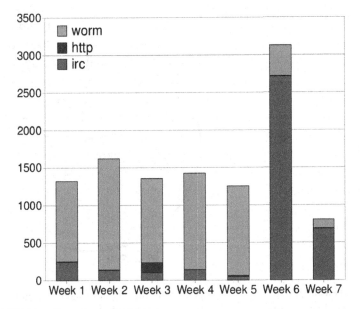

Fig. 7.8 Weekly collected samples per type

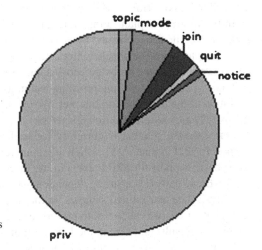

Fig. 7.9 Distribution of the IRC commands issued on the controlling channels

7.5   Conclusions and Future Work

We have proposed a new three-stage open honeypot architecture for malware data collection and analysis. We believe our solution, if widely deployed, could significantly ease the sharing of collected data. Our architecture is fully open: anyone can implement it using Open Source software and validate our results using the same platform. Moreover, the use of the OSI-approved GPL license encourages community contributions to the

Fig. 7.10 Breakdown of IRC commands by type

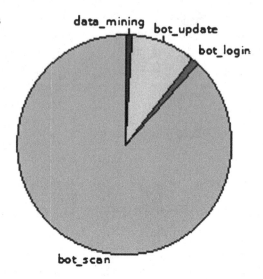

project, and ensure it will always stay open. With the help of Colajanni et al. from [10], we are currently evaluating the feasibility of integration of HIVE and their architecture. We believe this two works complement nicely and could lead to the development of a new and more powerful malware collection and analysis infrastructure.

In the future, we plan to integrate attack information into our database. Using, for example, the data collected by HoneyWall, would allow us to correlate the malware samples with the attack vectors they used to break into the system, giving a better overview of the malware ecosystem. The analysis of the attackers operating systems (via passive OS fingerprinting techniques) could also provide insight in the evolution of the underground Internet. We are also investigating PE Hunter [43] and Argos [27] as possible additional sensors.

Our database schema is currently focused on centralized botnets; there is no support for P2P botnets [15], which are an increasing threat. We plan to add at least some basic support for P2P botnets in the future.

HIVE currently has a strong dependency on CWSandbox – it's our main source of analysis data on captured samples. In the future, we plan to integrate more tightly several other analysis services, to provide a level of redundancy and cross-checking on analysis results and spread the load on multiple systems.

Finally, we will write a reporting interface to expose interesting data and trends in a user friendly way. We believe that the easy availability of aggregate data on malware threats will greatly help developing new countermeasures.

7.6 Availability

Implementation details for the HIVE platform, the database DDL and our programs source code are all available at http://netlab-mn.unipv.it/hive or through the authors. Future developments and data reports will be published at the same location.

References

1. F-Secure world map. http://worldmap.f-secure.com.
2. The honeynet project. http://www.honeynet.org.
3. Leurrecom.org honeypot project. http://www.leurrecom.org.
4. The mwcollect alliance. http://alliance.mwcollect.org.
5. Prelude hybrid IDS project. http://www.prelude-ids.com/en/development/.
6. Baecher P, Koetter M, Holz T, Dornseif M, Freiling F (2006) The Nepenthes platform: An efficient approach to collect malware. In Springer, editor, Proceedings of the 9th International Symposium on Recent Advances in Intrusion Detection (RAID), 165–184, Sept. 2006.
7. Balas E, Viecco C (2005) Towards a third generation data capture architecture for honeynets. In Systems, Man and Cybernetics (SMC) Information Assurance Workshop. Proceedings from the Sixth Annual IEEE, 21–28, June 15–17.
8. Bayer U, Moser A, Kruegel C, Kirda E. (2006) Dynamic analysis of malicious code. Journal in Computer Virology, 2(1):67–77.
9. Bellard F (2005) QEMU, a fast and portable dynamic translator. In Proceedings of the USENIX 2005 Annual Technical Conference, FREENIX Track, 41–46, June 2005.
10. Colajanni M, Gozzi D, Marchetti M (2008) Collaborative architecture for malware detection and analysis. In Proceedings of The IFIP TC 11 23rd International Information Security Conference, volume 278/2008 of IFIP International Federation for Information Processing, 79–93. Springer Boston, July 2008.
11. Dornseif M, Holz T, Klein CN (2004) NoSEBrEaK - attacking honeynets. In Information Assurance Workshop. Proceedings of the Fifth Annual IEEE SMC, 123–129, June 2004.
12. Göbel JG. Amun: Python honeypot. http://amunhoney.sourceforge.net.
13. Göbel JG (2007) Infiltrator v0.1. http://zeroq.kulando.de/post/2007/11/15/infiltrator_v01, Nov. 2007.
14. Göbel JG (2008) Infiltrator v0.3. http://zeroq.kulando.de/post/2008/10/20/infiltrator-v0.3, Oct. 2008.
15. Grizzard JB, Sharma V, Nunnery C, Kang BB, Dagon D (2007) Peer-to-peer botnets: overview and case study. In HotBots'07: Proceedings of the First Conference on First Workshop on Hot Topics in Understanding Botnets, 1–1, Berkeley, CA, USA, USENIX Association.
16. Hispasec Sistemas. Virustotal. http://www.virustotal.com.
17. Holz T, Raynal F (2005) Detecting honeypots and other suspicious environments. In Information Assurance Workshop, IAW '05. Proceedings of the Sixth Annual IEEE SMC, 29–36, June 2005.
18. International Secure Systems Lab. Anubis: Analyzing unknown binaries. http://anubis.iseclab.org.
19. Joe Security. Joebox. http://www.joebox.org/.
20. Leita C, Pham VH, Thonnard O, Ramirez ES, Pouget F, Kirda E, Dacier M (2008) The leurre. com project: Collecting internet threats information using a worldwide distributed honeynet. In Information Security Threats Data Collection and Sharing. WISTDCS '08. WOMBAT Workshop, 40–57, Amsterdam, Apr. 2008.
21. MaxMind. GeoLite City. http://www.maxmind.com/app/geolitecity.
22. McCanne S, Leres C, Jacobson V (2008) libpcap. http://www.tcpdump.org/.
23. Mukkamala S, Yendrapalli K, Basnet R, Shankarapani MK, Sung AH (2007) Detection of virtual environments and low interaction honeypots. In Information Assurance and Security Workshop. IAW '07. IEEE SMC, 92–98, West Point, NY, June 2007.
24. Norman. SandBox information center. http://sandbox.norman.no/.
25. Ormandy T (2007) An empirical study into the security exposure to hosts of hostile virtualized environments. Technical report, Google, Inc., Apr. 2007.
26. Porras P, Shmatikov V (2006) Large-scale collection and sanitization of network security data: risks and challenges. In NSPW '06: Proceedings of the 2006 Workshop on New security paradigms, 57–64, New York, NY, USA, ACM.
27. Portokalidis G, Slowinska A, Bos H (2006) Argos: an emulator for fingerprinting zero-day attacks. In Proc. ACM SIGOPS EUROSYS'2006, Leuven, Belgium, Apr. 2006.

28. Pouget F, Dacier M, Pham VH (2005) Leurre.com: on the advantages of deploying a large scale distributed honeypot platform. In ECCE'05, E-Crime and Computer Conference, 29-30th March 2005, Monaco.
29. Provos N (2004) A virtual honeypot framework. In Proceedings of the 13th USENIX Security Symposium, San Diego, CA, Aug. 2004.
30. Rajab MA, Zarfoss J, Monrose F, Terzis A (2006) A multifaceted approach to understanding the botnet phenomenon. In IMC '06: Proceedings of the 6th ACM SIGCOMM conference on Internet measurement, pages 41–52, New York, NY, USA. ACM.
31. Sophos (2008) W32/Allaple-B. http://www.sophos.com/security/analyses/viruses-and-spyware/ w32allapleb.html.
32. Sourcefire, Inc. Clam antiVirus. http://www.clamav.net.
33. SUN Microsystems. VirtualBox. http://www.virtualbox.org/.
34. Sunbelt. Cwsandbox. http://www.cwsandbox.org/.
35. The Artemis Team. HoneyBow. http://honeybow.mwcollect.org/.
36. The Honeynet project (2003) Know your enemy: Sebek. http://old.honeynet.org/papers/sebek. pdf, Aug. 2003.
37. The Honeynet project (2005) Know your enemy: Honeywall cdrom roo. http://www.honeynet. org/papers/cdrom/roo/index.html, Aug. 2005.
38. The Linux Foundation. Net:bridge. http://www.linux-foundation.org/en/Net:Bridge.
39. The PostgreSQL Global Development Group. Slony-I: enterprise-level replication system. http://slony.info/.
40. The PostgreSQL Global Development Group PostgreSQL 8.3.1 documentation. appendix D. SQL conformance. http://www.postgresql.org/docs/8.3/static/features.html, Mar. 2008.
41. Trend Micro (2007) Threat report and forecast. Technical report, Trend Micro.
42. Werner T. Honeytrap. http://honeytrap.mwcollect.org/.
43. Werner T. PE hunter. http://honeytrap.mwcollect.org/pehunter.
44. Willems C, Holz T, Freiling F (2007) Toward Automated Dynamic Malware Analysis Using CWSandbox. IEEE Security & Privacy Magazine, 5(2):32–39.
45. Zhuge J, Holz T, Han X, Song C, Zou W (2007) Collecting autonomous spreading malware using high-interaction honeypots. In ICICS 2007, 438–451.
46. Zou CC, Cunningham R (2006) Honeypot-aware Advanced Botnet Construction and Maintenance. International Conference on Dependable Systems and Networks, 199–208, Philadelphia, PA.

Chapter 8
Selective File Dumper

Nanni Bassetti and Denis Frati

Abstract During a computer forensics investigation we faced a problem how to get all the interesting files we need fast. We work, mainly, using the Open Source software products and Linux OS, and we consider the Sleuthkit and the Foremost two very useful tools, but for reaching our target they were too complicated and time consuming to use. For this reason we developed the Selective File Dumper, a Linux Bash script which makes it possible to extract all the referenced, deleted and unallocated files and finally to perform a keyword search, in a simple way.

8.1 Introduction

Open Source [15, 17] approach in software development is based on a premise that sharing knowledge, inventions and discoveries is vital to progress of the mankind. Those who develop software in the Open Source community do not wish to protect their creation, on the contrary, they intend to make a contribution to the others; they also believe that the cooperation will help improve their ideas.

Another advantage is that, often, the ideas, the projects and the actual development takes place on the Internet, among persons whose don't know each other physically. They may be found all over the world, unhindered by office location or working hours.

During a computer forensic investigation, using **Linux Kubuntu 7.10** [8] and all the open source computer forensics tool like **Autopsy** [7] and **Sleuthkit** [1, 9], **Foremost** [10], etc. we needed to find information probably included in DOC, PDF

N. Bassetti (✉)
Via Della Costituente, 37 – 70125 Bari, Italy
e-mail: nannib@libero.it

D. Frati
Via A. Testa, 16 – 10010 Banchette (TO), Italy
e-mail: denis.frati@cybercrimes.it

E. Huebner and S. Zanero (eds.), *Open Source Software for Digital Forensics*,
DOI 10.1007/978-1-4419-5803-7_8, © Springer Science+Business Media, LLC 2010

and BMP files and the device under investigation was about 200 Gb. We tried the keyword search, but we didn't know what exactly what we were searching for, because our Warrant was generic. For this reason, we needed to export and save all referenced and deleted files (DOC, PDF and BMP) manually, in a directory called "Evidences", in order to give all these files to the prosecutor for the examination.

Following the Open Source philosophy, we developed a new tool "**Selective File Dumper**", and we published it on Sourgeforce [14], the biggest Open Source web community at the URL http://sfdumper.sourceforge.net. Without the Selective File Dumper, the only way to reach all the targets above is to enter many Sleuthkit and Linux commands on the command line, but even then the results are not as good.

With mounting the image many problems are easier to solve, but to maintain the best practice of computer forensics science it is always better not to mount any images or devices. Anyway often it is impossible to mount [2, 3, 4, 5, 6].

For this reason, in order to reach the target of extracting all the referenced, deleted and unallocated files by their extension, without mounting the device or the image file, many tools like MMLS,FLS, ICAT, GREP, AWK, FOREMOST, SED and other Linux native tools [1, 8, 9, 10] are very difficult to use. For example, the carving operation extracts all the files present on the image file or the device examined, including the referenced and the deleted files.

We realised that many investigators have this problem, so, in order to solve it, we decided to build a software tool that could extract all the file types automatically. It could have the feature to carve the files from the entire partition selected, deleting the duplicated files and leaving only the carved ones which are not present in the referenced or deleted sets of files. Finally the tool could do a keyword search on all the files (referenced, deleted, carved). To start the project we chose the following software products to use in our Bash Script [12, 16]:

- Sleuthkit – for retrieving referenced and deleted files
- Foremost – for the data carving
- Sha256deep – for creating the hash numbers of the referenced, deleted and carved files.
- Grep – for the keyword search
- Awk – for parsing the output of the above software products
- Sed – for parsing the output of the above software products
- DD – for inputing the partition bit stream to Foremost.

The project was based on an interactive **Linux Bash Script**, using all open sources software products, extensively tested and accepted by the computer forensics community. For automating many manual operations, the output would be only in one of four directories:

1. Referenced files,
2. Deleted files,
3. Carved files,
4. Report and logs.

The first obstacle we came across was the correct recognition of the file system and the partitions. We used **mmls** and **fsstat** (Sleuthkit) to determine if there is a file system on the image file or device we are analyzing. Thanks to the combination of these two powerful tools we can have one of three outcomes:

1. There is no file system or partition (among these recognized by the Sleuthkit) – only data carving is possible.
2. There is a strange partition starting from the ZERO sector – it could be a partition.
3. There are file systems and partitions and it is possible to choose what do you want to analyze.

For the cases number **2** and **3** we used the **fls** and **icat** (Sleuthkit) to extract all the referenced and the deleted files from the partition we choose.

The Selective File Dumper (SfDumper) is a tool that allows for the recovery of files; very useful for the operator who intends to work with the information stored in the files (the text of the document, the contents of image files) and not on control information about the files, like metadata. The metadata is still recoverable for individual files, using the information included in the logs, in particular the path, the file name and its inode.

8.2   The Script in Action

We can launch the script in two ways by entering the following command in the terminal window:

sudo sh sfdumper.sh   or   *chmod +x sfdumper.sh./sfdumper.sh*

When the script starts we can see a menu and we can RUN the process, as shown in Fig. 8.1.

First we must insert the *"Investigator's name"*, then we must indicate the output directory for the retrieved files and the reports. Secondly we must indicate the image file or the device (eg. /dev/sdb) to analyse. At this point we could have the **mmls** output as shown in Fig. 8.2.

We choose a partition by entering its number eg. "**02**", then we must enter the file type we need, for example doc, jpg, pdf etc.

In the output directory we will see a directory named in the following way:

partition_NumberOfThePartitionChose__fileType
eg: **partition_02__pdf**

In the case when there is no file system, it is a raw image files or device, we will see a directory named in the folling way:

image__fileType
eg.: **image__pdf**

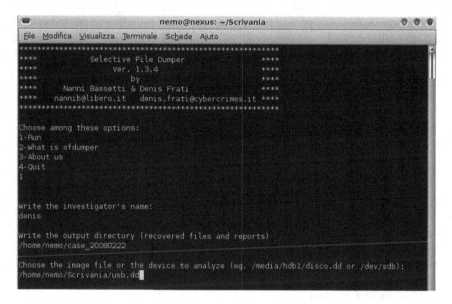

Fig. 8.1 The starting menu

Inside these directories we will find others directories: deleted_files_recovered, referenced_files_recovered, carvingFileType (eg. carvingpdf), Report etc., as shown in Fig. 8.3. The content of these directories is obvious.

The file names will be composed in the following way:

corresponding **inode_path_filename** with the spaces replaced by "_" (underscore) and the slashes replaced by "-" (dash).

Eg: **1994280_My_Documents-story.doc**

After to have indicate the file type we could choose if we would like to do a data carving, in affirmative case the script will use the power of the **Foremost** and **DD**.

The script, using the Linux pipe "**|**" operator, will input only the chosen partition bit stream to the Foremost in the following way, where **$imm** is the partition, and **$carv_dir** is the output carving directory:

$$dd\ if=\$imm\ conv=noerror,sync|foremost-t\$2-o\$carv\_dir;$$

or

$$dd\ if=\$imm\ conv=noerror,sync|foremost-c\$dir\_outputtmp/carving$$
$$\_config.txt-o\$carv\_dir$$

The script automatically creates a Foremost configuration file named "*carving_config.txt*" in the "tmp" directory inside the output directory we choose, so it can use all the build-in Foremost recognized extensions or, if the file type is not among these, it can use the configuration file.

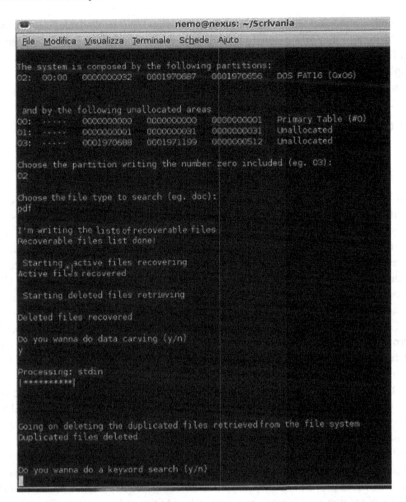

Fig. 8.2 mmls output and the other operations

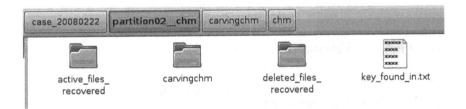

Fig. 8.3 Directories

Another important feature is that the configuration file is expandable; it is possible to add many other file extensions and their related "magic numbers", headers and footers which identify the file type, just by editing the sfdumper.sh script by a simple text editor.

Here is a sample of the *carving_config.txt* file for the headers of Outlook Express file :

Outlook Express
dbx y 4000000 \xcf\xad\x12\xfe\xc5\xfd\x74\x6f
idx y 4000000 \x4a\x4d\x46\x39
mbx y 4000000 \x4a\x4d\x46\x36

If we choose to do the data carving, all files will be carved, including the referenced and the deleted files. We don't need them, we need only the carved files not belonging to the referenced and deleted files sets. For this reason, the script will execute the **Sha256deep** [11] hashing function on all the carved files and on all the referenced and deleted files, then it will compare the hash numbers and it will delete the duplicated files in the carved file set. The Sha256 hash algorithm has been chosen because, currently, it has fewer collision problems, so it is safer than MD5.

Carving the files is a useful approach, because we can discover the renamed files. For example if one file was named **terrorist_plan.doc** and it was renamed to **terrorist_plan.gfx**, then the script executing the search for the file type "doc", will not find it, neither in the referenced files nor in the deleted files, but Foremost, using the files headers for carving, will correctly recognize it as a DOC file.

After the data carving request, the script will ask for a keyword search. In this case we used the powerful tool **grep**, so the script will search, recursively, all the referenced, deleted and carved files, with the keyword chosen, and it will write the file names, containing the keyword, into a log file called **key_found.txt**.

All the operations and the file lists are reported in some log files in the directory **"Report"**. The **main_log.txt** is the main log file containing the starting/ending date and time of the process, the investigator's name, the names of the files containing the lists of referenced, deleted and carved files. At the end the script will ask if you want to conduct another analysis, so it is possible to search for different file types and in different partitions.

8.3   The GUI Version

We also developed a GUI version of Selective File Dumper, using the Zenity graphics libraries. From Zenity web site [13]:

"Zenity is a tool that allows you to display Gtk+ dialog boxes from the command line and through shell scripts. It is similar to gdialog, but is intended to be saner. It comes from the same family as dialog, Xdialog, and cdialog, but it surpasses those projects by having a cooler name."

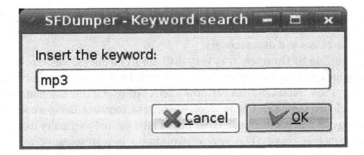

Fig. 8.4 SFDumper GUI Menu

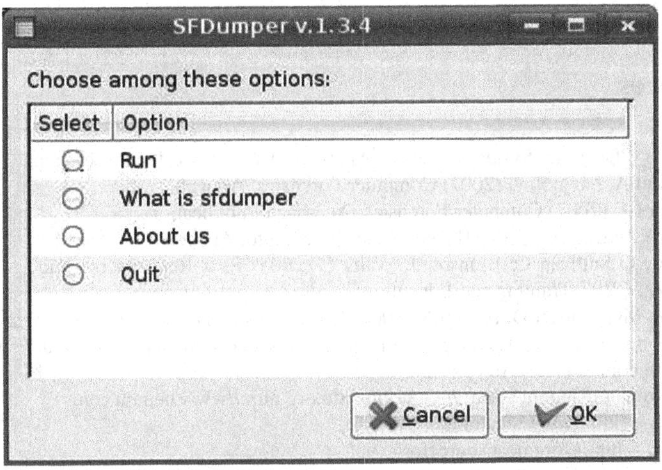

Fig. 8.5 The keyword search dialog window

The GUI version of SFDumper has been improved in order to provide a better human interface, but it needs another third part software product i.e. Zenity. The examples of the GUI interface are shown in figure 8.4 and figure 8.5.

The advantage of the shell version versus the GUI version is that the shell version can run directly from the Linux **runlevel 2**; this means the script runs also from a Linux distribution with the command line only interface.

8.4   Conclusion

Creating SFDumper was hard work, motivated by an actual need. To the best of our knowledge there is no other software product with comparable functionality, at least in the Open Source world. Although individually these are simple operations, before **Selective File Dumper**, they all had to be performed manually, which is both tedious and error prone. We hope this product will help many operators of computer forensics and data recovery.

Without using **SFDumper**, it is very difficult to obtain the same results every time using the command line only. This is why we developed this interactive script, which after a few questions, can perform a series of operations automatically.

We developed our project in an Open Source environment, using a collaborative methodology. We never met each other physically, but only virtually using Skype, e-mail and mobile phone. This way of working it is representative of the Open Source philosophy, which is oriented towards the knowledge sharing and the delocalization. We hope to receive feedback and suggestions from users and developers, for improving our project and for developing new ideas.

References

1. Carrier B (2005) File System Forensics Analysis. Addison Wesley Professional
2. Ghirardini A, Faggioli G (2007) Computer Forensics. Apogeo
3. Newman RC (2007) Computer Forensics. Auerbach Pubblications
4. Mandia K, Prosise C (2002) Hacker Pronto Intervento. Apogeo
5. Nolan R, O'Sullivan C, Branson J, Waits C (2005) First Responders Guide to Computer Forensics. CERT Training and Education
6. Solomon MG, Barrett D, Broom N (2005) Computer Forensics JumpStart. Sybex
7. Autopsy and Sleuthkit. The Digital Forensics Toolkit. The Tracker Dog's Guide www.linux-magazine.com/issue/36/Autopsy.pdf
8. Linux Kubuntu/Ubuntu – http://www.kubuntu.org http://www.ubuntu.com
9. Sleuthkit – http://www.sleuthkit.org
10. Foremost – http://foremost.sourceforge.net
11. Sha256deep – http://md5deep.sourceforge.net/
12. Bash Guide – http://tldp.org/LDP/abs/html/
13. Zenity - http://freshmeat.net/projects/zenity
14. Sourceforge – http://sourceforge.net
15. Wikipedia - http://en.wikipedia.org/wiki/Open_source
16. Bash Cookbook - Carl Albing, JP Vossen, Cameron Newham – O'Reilly – 2007
17. Producing Open Source Software: How to Run a Successful Free Software Project -Karl Fogel – O'Reilly - Paperback 2005